CARO'S FUNDAMENTAL SECRETS OF WINNING POKER

**New Edition!
A Poker Classic!**

"There are more insights on winning at poker in this book than any I've ever read. An absolute must for any poker player."
Avery Cardoza, the world's foremost authority on gambling

"Mike Caro has taught more players to win than anyone in history! His research and seminars have totally revolutionized poker."
Doyle Brunson, two-time world champion, world's best poker player

"Much more than a world-class poker player, Caro provides the most powerful, sought-after, and scientific winning advice ever put on paper."
Scott Rogers, president Card Player, the leading magazine for poker players

To Phyllis, who's really fantastic, and to our son, Silver–possibly the smartest African Grey parrot . . .

ABOUT THE AUTHOR

"The father of modern poker," Mike Caro, was born in 1944. Today he lives in Los Angeles with his wife Phyllis – a well-known casino executive – and his cockatoo parrot, Powder. Known alternatively as "The Mad Genius of Poker," "America's Mad Genius," "Gambling's Mad Genius," or just "The Mad Genius," Caro has devoted much of his life to analyzing poker and making his latest research available to the public through his standing-room-only seminars. His high-energy, easy-to-follow method of teaching is reflected in his books, articles, columns, and videos.

Besides this book, he is the author of *Caro on Gambling, Poker for Women-A Course in Destroying Male Opponents at Poker and Beyond, Caro's Fundamental Secrets of Poker, New Poker Games, Gambling Times Quiz Book, Bobby Baldwin's Winning Poker Secrets, Mike Caro's Guide to Doyle Brunson's Super/System – A Course in Power Poker,* and many limited-edition reports aimed at poker professionals. Additionally, he was an expert collaborator for the *Brunson Super/System,* often considered the bible of poker, and has had over 400 articles and columns published about poker.

In 1983, he personally programmed his computer, Orac (Caro spelled backwards), to play no-limit, heads-up hold'em at a world-class level. Though Orac lost a nationally televised match for a $500,000 prize, the project astounded the computer, scientific, and poker worlds. The consensus was that, indeed, Orac could play at a world-class level 16 years ago, and it even won one of its three matches at the World Series of Poker™ against a world champion. Today, with better computers and more innovations, Caro believes that a soon-to-be-reincarnated Orac will play significantly better than any human alive, including himself.

Mike Caro has long fought for the integrity of poker, founding his Cheater Monitoring Service almost 20 years ago. Today that same service, which takes reports on unethical behavior and strives to maintain the honesty and dignity of poker, is an integral part Mike Caro University (MCU).

Mike Caro believes that your main task in life is to make better and better decisions. Without information, he points out, you can't know the odds or adjust your decisions rationally. That's the message behind his most famous quote, which has appeared in everything from gambling magazines to Newsweek: "In the beginning, everything was even-money."

MIKE CARO UNIVERSITY

Housed within Hollywood Park-Casino, Mike Caro University of Poker, Gaming and Life Strategy (MCU) merges Caro's own research with the collective wisdom of other great poker minds to form a one-of-a-kind learning center teaching poker strategy and psychology. In addition to instructional courses, MCU serves as a central force for popularizing poker, maintaining its integrity, and standardizing rules. (Website: UniversityofPoker.com)

To join the MCU mailing list: join@caro.com
To contact the author: caro@caro.com

CARO'S FUNDAMENTAL SECRETS OF WINNING POKER

Mike Caro

The Mad Genius of Poker

This Cardoza edition is printed by special arrangement with Mike Caro University of Poker Press.

MIKE ♠ CARO

MCU
UNIVERSITY

The Advanced School of Winning!
POKER • GAMING • LIFE STRATEGY

Cardoza Publishing

Cardoza Publishing is the foremost gaming and gambling publisher in the world with a library of almost 100 up-to-date and easy-to-read books and strategies. These authoritative works are written by the top experts in their fields and with more than 7,000,000 books in print, represent the best-selling and most popular gaming books anywhere.

THIRD EDITION

| First Printing | September 2002 |
| Second Printing | April 2004 |

Copyright ©1991, 1996, 2002 by Mike Caro
- All Rights Reserved -

Library of Congress Catalog No: 2002101912
ISBN: 1-58042-080-X

This Cardoza edition this book is printed by special arrangement with Mike Caro University of Poker Press. You may use up to 250 words in any copyrighted review, book, commentary or article if you attribute the quoted material to *Caro's Fundamental Secrets of Winning Poker*, and its author, Mike Caro.

Visit our new web site (www.cardozapub.com) or write us for a full list of books, advanced and computer strategies.

CARDOZA PUBLISHING

PO Box 1500 Cooper Station, New York, NY 10276
Toll Free Phone (800)577-WINS
email: cardozapub@aol.com
www.cardozapub.com

TABLE OF CONTENTS

1. Introduction

There is no good reason you shouldn't win consistently at poker. Winning is easy. Sure, it's **not** easy if you treat poker like bingo. It's **not** easy if you treat poker primarily as a game of luck. If you do that, don't bother even sitting at the table–you might as well mail in your money. But if you treat poker with the respect it deserves, you'll win. Nothing else is possible.

Originally, I called this *Caro's Poker Seminar Playbook*. But I found myself explaining many ideas in more detail than I do at most seminars. So, while this book is based largely on my seminar teachings, it also emphasizes some little-known concepts that are easier to explain in print. These seldom-analyzed topics comprise the very foundation of poker theory.

Put simply, *Caro's Fundamental Secrets of Winning Poker* captures the most important concepts I teach at my live seminars–and more. If you've ever attended, you know that we put a heavy emphasis on motivation. That's because so many potentially pro-level players fail to win at poker. They come to the poker table armed with insight and information and logic. They have all the tools anyone ever needed to beat poker. Yet they're losers.

Why do these poker players fail? Often, it's not because they're unaware of the right tactics or techniques. Many players have studied poker and know a great deal. Many players have years and years of experience and possess a good feel for the game. Still, they don't win. And the reason they don't win is simply that they don't play their best game all the time.

At my poker seminars, we talk about those emotional traps we all encounter–traps that can keep us from winning. In addition, we discuss important strategic concepts. There are occasional statistics and examples of how to play hands for many specific kinds of poker.

In this book, I'll present the same concepts, motivational advice–plus a few statistics and some of the best strategy–you'd experience at a live seminar. But wait! Although this book covers much valuable territory, I still think you'd find it worthwhile coming to a seminar in person. In fact, I'd feel honored if you'd bring this book with you.

If you decide to attend a live seminar, you'll see important concepts projected on a screen while I explain them. For this book, what you'd normally see on that screen will, instead, appear on a blackboard like this . . .

> **Important concepts that would be projected on a screen at my live seminars appear on a blackboard in this book.**

Okay, it looks like you got here early and found a good seat. So, I'm ready to get started anytime you are.

2. Why You Really Can Beat Poker!

Think back to the day you were born. Remember? No? Okay, I'll tell you how it was. Your head was remarkably empty, no seeds were scattered on your farm, and no chalk marks blemished your blackboard. Got it?

There you were in the year of y*ou-fill-in-the-blank*. You didn't know anything yet. You see, at that moment I could have told you that a cow named Robert was President of *The Known Universe* and you would have simply thought, "Hey, that sounds like a good possibility! Maybe you're telling me the truth and maybe you aren't. It's fifty-fifty." Reality, my friends, is a coin flip until you learn otherwise.

That brings us to the primary truth that governs both poker and the real world beyond poker.

> **In the beginning, everything was even money.**

Those simple words open the gate. Beyond the gate is a path. Scattered along the path, buried beneath the leaves and the litter, are clues. Clues everywhere. These are *your* clues, and they let *you* understand life's path. Each clue helps you challenge the assumption that an event is even money.

Now don't get lost. Follow what I'm saying. This is the most important concept governing your destiny that you can ever master. It is, far and away, the most powerful way of looking at life.

When you were just born, I could have told you that cars fly. And someone else might have told you that, no, it's airplanes that fly. And you wouldn't have had the slightest idea who was right. It would have been just another coin flip to you. Yes, just another coin flip. Exactly even money, like everything else.

But the more you learn as you walk down life's path, the more you are able to use the clues you gather to decide whether something really is even money. No trucks coming? Looks safe to cross the street, right? You don't really bother to put it in words, but what you're really saying is the chances of safely getting to the other side are 2,999 out of 3,000 or 999,999 out of 1,000,000–we all set our own standards for acceptable risk. The point is, hardly anyone would cross the street if the odds of getting successfully to the other side were only two out of three. That would mean that if you crossed just two streets, you'd probably be dead. So, intelligent people instinctively see that having a 2-to-1 favorable advantage is not enough to cross a street.

Where is this leading? It's leading to the powerful truth that the better you are at determining how things around you affect your chances, the more successful you'll be. That's so important that I'm going to repeat it. The truth is that the better you can decide how everything around you affects your chances, the more success you'll enjoy.

Gambling is no different. In gambling, you've got to decide rationally how people, things, and events affect your chances of winning. Whether instinctively or actually by calculating odds on paper, intelligent people always develop skills that help them estimate their chances of success. The key element of success is knowing what your chances are and planning strategy accordingly. Listen one more time. Success is simply knowing what your chances are and then planning your strategy.

But can knowing your chances and planning your strategy help you win at gambling? Good question. The answer is yes, but only at some kinds of gambling. There are certain games you can't beat, no matter what.

> **The key to winning. In order to overcome the odds against you at gambling, your decisions must really matter.**

You're just wasting your time trying to beat a game if your decisions don't matter. By "matter" I mean that your decisions must make a difference from some logical point of view. Just looking back at a coin flip that landed tails and saying, "It's clear I should've called tails," is **not** a logical point of view. Why? Because before that coin flip, you had no informed reason to pick tails over heads. Your decision didn't really matter *beforehand*.

When I say that your decisions must matter in order to overcome the odds *against* you gambling, I'm not forgetting that the odds could be *in your favor* from the start. If that's the case, if someone is giving you an overlay or you're assuming the house edge at craps against other players, then you're going to win eventually, even though your decisions don't matter.

Normally, though, for most gamblers, having a house advantage *on their side* is out of the question. Typically, we face situations where the odds are neutral or where the odds are against us, but good decision-making can make those more favorable. Even if your decisions matter, it doesn't mean you're going to win. Take horses, for instance; thoroughbred handicapping. Maybe you've got some skills, but only enough to trim your disadvantage from 17% down to 11%. You're still going to lose eventually. Horse handicapping is a great example of a type of gambling where you *can* win, but you need extremely high skills and solid information.

What about craps and roulette? Do your decisions really matter? No. That's why you'll meet a few professional sports bettors and some professional blackjack players. But in the whole world there is not one professional craps shooter! At least, not if the game is honest and the odds are against the shooter.

In poker, do your decisions really matter? They do, don't they? It matters whether you call or throw a hand away, whether you raise or just call, whether you bet or check. These decisions usually are not merely coin flips; they are not even money. It is your skill and your judgment that will decide your fate.

Who wins? In poker, good players beat bad players.

Think about that. In poker, the money goes from the weak players to the strong players. Surely you've heard that you can't win gambling. Maybe your Aunt Rosalie told you that or your Uncle Ned. Guess what? Somebody's got to win gambling. Maybe it's the casino or a bookie or some guy with an edge. I repeat, somebody's got to win gambling–otherwise, where would the money go? In poker, a game of skill, the money flows from the bad players to the strong players. It's as simple as that.

> **In the long run. In poker, you don't get paid to win pots–you get paid to make the right decisions.**

One of the saddest and most costly poker attitudes is that the object is to win pots. Look, right now as you read this–everywhere on Earth–the players who are *winning the most pots* are *losing the most money*. That's so important that I'm going to repeat it: All across America, those who win the most pots lose the most money.

How come? Think about it this way: If you stubbornly decided you would never throw a hand away from now on, what would happen? You'd win just about every pot you could possibly win, right? You'd never pass, you'd call every bet, and you'd win more pots than anyone else. But what would that bring you? Disaster! You'd simply run out of money quickly, because you wouldn't win enough pots to balance the expense.

Sure, you can argue that you *could* play even worse than that. You could call almost every time except the last bet, for instance. Then you'd never win a pot and you'd lose even more money than someone who called every bet. Interesting argument, but that's not how it really happens. There really are players who call almost every bet. There really are players who see far too many showdowns. And these are the biggest losers in poker.

So, obviously, the object of poker isn't to win pots–the object is to invest your money wisely. In poker, you get paid to make quality decisions, not to win pots.

> **The main reason people fail to accomplish as much as they could–in poker and in life–is <u>they don't play their best game always.</u>**

One other warning now. There's hardly a player alive that plays his best game all the time. Poker is frustrating. You lose a pot you should have won, an opponent beats you on a poor percentage play, you go three hours without making a flush. All these things are frustrating. In response to frustration–or sometimes simply for adventure–we tend to stray from the proven profitable strategy we know will win. We play worse than we are capable.

You can't afford to do that anymore! I know of hundreds of players who are good at reading opponents and who know the correct strategy. But they're not playing today. They're home sulking. Sulking because they lacked the ability to play their best game all the time. Is 50% of the time enough? Of course not. How about 75% of the time. No, that won't get the money. In fact, even 99% of the time may not be enough. It depends, of course, on how big an advantage you have over your opponents and how much you throw away in bad decisions when you don't play your best game. So, by saying 99% isn't enough, I'm also telling you that you *must* play your best game all the time. Make yourself a promise right now: *I will play my best game all the time.*

3. How to Play Poker

In a way, I hate to add this chapter to *Fundamental Secrets of Winning Poker*. Sure, for many readers, this will be a useful chapter, and even experienced players may want to refer to it now and then. But most day-in and day-out players already understand what's here. Other chapters in this book are about tips, tactics, and concepts that help you win at the poker table. This one is different.

You can't take it to the bank from here. You can't ponder here; you can't add weapons to your poker arsenal here. There are no blackboards here. Instead, this is the place where I'm going to define the most basic procedures of poker. Here is how the games are played.

I've divided these procedures into four sections, corresponding to these games: Draw poker, hold 'em, seven-card stud, and seven-card high-low split.

First, you need to know that every traditional poker hands consists of five cards and that the 52 cards are individually identifiable by two features: rank and suit. There are 13 different possible ranks: ace (highest), king, queen, jack, 10, 9, 8, 7, 6, 5, 4, 3, and 2 (also called "deuce," lowest).

Here is a handy listing of which hands are higher and, therefore, beat less-powerful hands below. Sure, you probably already know this, but here's the damn chart, anyway. Share it with someone you love…

FIVE-CARD POKER HAND VALUES
(Applicable to almost all poker games where high hand wins)

Hands are listed in descending order from the strongest, the Royal Flush, to the weakest, no pair hands.

ROYAL FLUSH *Example:* A♣ K♣ Q♣ J♣ 10♣
Described: Five cards of consecutive ranks from ace down to ten, all the same suit. (Royal Flush is merely the best Straight Flush.)
Ties: Two or more Royal Flushes divide the pot.

STRAIGHT FLUSH *Example:* 9♦ 8♦ 7♦ 6♦ 5♦
Described: Five cards of consecutive ranks, all the same suit. (Ace can be used low to form a five-high Straight Flush.)
Ties: Higher ranking Straight wins. (Rank of Straight is the rank of the card that begins the downward sequence.)

FOUR OF A KIND *Example:* 3♣ 3♦ 3♥ 3♠ K♣
Described: Four cards of a matching rank, plus an extra card.
Ties: Higher rank of the Four of a Kind wins. Extra card doesn't matter.

FULL HOUSE *Example:* 9♣ 9♥ 9♠ Q♦ Q♠
Described: Three cards of matching rank, plus two cards of a different matching rank.
Ties: Higher rank of the Three of a Kind within the Full House wins. Extra pair doesn't matter.

FLUSH *Example:* A♠ J♠ 7♠ 6♠ 2♠
Described: Five cards of the same suit that do not qualify as a Straight Flush or Royal Flush.
Ties: Highest ranking card wins. If those are the same, next highest card wins, and so forth.

STRAIGHT *Example:* 8♦ 7♠ 6♦ 5♣ 4♥
Described: Five ranks in sequence. (Ace can be used low to form a five-high Straight.)
Ties: Higher rank beginning the sequence wins.

THREE OF A KIND *Example:* A♦ A♣ A♥ Q♦ 4♠
Described: Three cards of a matching rank and two extra cards whose ranks do not match.
Ties: Higher rank of the Three of a Kind wins. Extra two cards don't matter.

TWO PAIR *Example:* K♥ K♦ 4♥ 4♦ A♠
Described: Two cards of a matching rank, plus two cards of another matching rank, plus one extra card.
Ties: Highest pair wins. If tied, higher second pair wins. If still tied, higher extra card wins.

ONE PAIR *Example:* 7♠ 7♥ Q♥ 10♠ 3♣
Described: Two cards of a matching rank, plus three extra cards of all different ranks.
Ties: Higher pair wins. If pairs rank the same, highest ranking extra card *not matched by opponent* wins.

NO PAIR *Example:* Q♥ J♠ 8♥ 6♦ 2♠
Described: Any hand that does not qualify for one of the categories listed above.
Ties: Highest card wins. If the hands tie for high card, the second highest cards are compared, and so forth.

Remember, the order that your poker cards are arranged in doesn't matter: 9♥ 10♦ Q♦ 8♣ J♠ is exactly the same as Q♦ J♠ 10♦ 9♥ 8♣. It makes no difference whether you go to the trouble of sorting your cards or not; you still have a straight.

Oh, and one other thing–the ace is not always the highest rank. Sometimes it can be used as the smallest card in this straight or straight flush: 5-4-3-2-A. Five-high is the *worst* straight you can get, and it doesn't beat the 6-5-4-3-2 straight, even though it contains an ace.

In describing the way these games are played, I have selected procedures that are simple and common. You might encounter slight variations, though. Maybe cutting the cards isn't required, or maybe one player antes for everyone. But usually, these games are conducted in a manner very similar to what I've described.

If you're unfamiliar with poker procedures, be sure to read the following section on draw poker, because some terminology is explained and those explanations are not repeated later. The procedures presented here are simplified, and I don't go into advanced rules like those covering "side pots" (when a player has less money than needed to call a bet), whether or not the dealer should "burn" before distributing cards, or what happens if you run out of cards. Things like this will vary from game to game, and it's best to ask the other players or the casino management if you're interested.

Simplified Draw Procedures

Maximum number of participants: 8.

Unless you've never played poker before, you probably already know how to play old-fashioned five-card draw. Draw poker is *real* poker. Draw poker is *pure* poker. It gives us that bet-the-ranch excitement you see all the time in those classic old-West movies.

You're dealt five cards. You get a chance to bet. You keep the cards you like and get replacements for the rest. You get a second chance to bet. If more than one player remains after this second and final betting round, the contestants turn their cards face up to determine the winner. That's called a **showdown**. Want more specifics?

We'll use a $5 and $10 betting limit as our example.

All players at your table **ante** by placing a mandatory token bet before receiving any cards. In our example game with $5 and $10 limits, each player antes $1. (The betting structure and limits used throughout this section serve only as an example. You'll encounter different betting limits and ante structures as well.)

1. The dealer shuffles. This might be a non-participating house dealer paid by a casino. In most home games, players take turns dealing, and after every hand the task passes to the left. This means you must deal when it's your turn.

2. The dealer offers the cut to a player on the right. Cards must be cut–at least five cards deep, leaving no fewer than five cards on the bottom.

3. The dealer distributes one card at a time face down to each player (self included, if participating), beginning to the left and continuing clockwise. The deal continues until each player has five cards.

4. There is now an initial round of betting. Beginning to the left of the dealer, each player looks at his hand and decides what to do. In old-fashioned "guts-to-open" poker, there are no minimum requirements to make the initial bet of $5 (known as **opening the pot**), so you can bet on raw courage if you want to. But if you're playing the popular variation called *jacks-or-better*, you need a least a pair of jacks to open for $5.

5. If the pot has already been opened by someone else when the action reaches you, you may **fold** (throw your hand away),

call (match the $5 bet), or **raise** (call the $5 bet *and* bet an additional $5, for a total of $10). If the pot has not already been opened, *you* can open or **check** (wait to see what other players do, reserving the option to call or raise if someone else bets). If you're the last person to act (known as the **dealer position**) and nobody has opened, you can check also, and the hand will end without a winner. Then the next hand is dealt, sometimes with a second $1 ante per player added to make the pot more enticing.

6. If there is **action,** meaning someone has opened, all bets are added to the pot, along with the original antes, in the center of the table.

7. If you bet or raise and all your opponents fold, you win what's in the pot, and there is no subsequent draw or betting.

8. If two or more players remain after the first round of betting, the deal continues and each remaining player, in turn–beginning at the dealer's left–can take replacements in an attempt to improve a hand. You may discard from one to all five unwanted cards and immediately be dealt new ones. Or you can **stand pat**–meaning you're satisfied with the cards you already have and don't want any replacements.

9. There is a second and final round of betting, beginning with the player who opened the pot. All bets are by the pre-established limits, double the amount of the bets on the first round of betting. So, since all bets on the first round were by increments of $5, all bets on the second round will be by increments of $10. If no one has bet when the action reaches you, you have the option of checking.

10. If you bet or raise and there is no call, the hand is over and you automatically win without a showdown.

11. If two or more players remain after the second and final betting round, there is a **showdown** to determine the winner. Players turn their cards face up on the table, and the best hand wins all the money in the pot. As in all these games, if two or more players tie with the best hands, then the pot is split equally among the winners.

12. Everyone antes for the next hand, and the process is repeated.

Simplified Seven-Card Stud Procedures

Maximum number of participants: Usually 7, but sometimes 8.

Seven-card stud poker is arguably the most widely played form of poker in America today. It differs from draw poker, where all cards remain your secret until the showdown, in that some cards are dealt face down for only you to look at, while others are dealt face up to be examined by everyone.

In all, if the hand doesn't terminate prematurely because a bet is uncalled, seven cards will be dealt to the players–three face down and four face up.

1. All players at your table ante by placing a mandatory token bet before receiving any cards. In our example game with $5 and $10 limits, each player antes $1. (You'll also encounter other betting limits and ante structures.)

2. The dealer shuffles. This might be a non-participating house dealer paid by a casino. In most home games, players take turns dealing, and after every hand the task passes to the left. This means you must deal when it's your turn.

3. The dealer offers the cut to a player on the right. Cards must be cut–at least five cards deep, leaving no fewer than five cards on the bottom.

4. The dealer distributes one card at a time face down to each player (self included, if participating), beginning to the left and continuing clockwise, until each participant has three cards. The first two cards dealt to each player are face down and are looked at only by the player of the hand; the third is face up.

5. The lowest-ranking **door card** (the term used for the first card dealt face up to the players) is forced to make a token starting bet, called the **bring in** bet, of $2. (Note that the size of the bring in bet will vary at different betting limits and games.) If two or more cards tie for lowest rank, the "low" suit determines the player that must make the bet. Even though no suit is worth more than another in poker, for this rare tie-breaking, who-bets-first purpose, the lowest rank is clubs, followed by diamonds, hearts, and then spades (alphabetical order).

6. Beginning with the player to the left of the $2 starting bet, each player must *call* the previous bet, "complete" it to the first $5 level, *raise* it $5 if the bet is already at least $5, or *fold*, throw the hand away.

7. All bets are added to the pot, along with the original antes, in the center of the table.

8. If you bet or raise and all your opponents fold, you win what's in the pot, and there is no subsequent draw or betting.

9. If two or more players remain after the first round of betting, the deal continues. The dealer delivers a fourth card, face up, to each remaining player, in turn–beginning at his left.

10. There is a second round of betting, beginning with the player who has the highest-ranking exposed (face up) card. If two players have high cards of that same rank, the higher-ranking second card determines who acts first. If *both* cards rank the same, the player nearest to the dealer's left acts first. All bets remain at the pre-established $5 limits.

11. If two or more players remain after the second round of betting, the deal continues. The dealer delivers a fifth card, face up, to each remaining player, in turn–beginning at his left.

12. There is a third round of betting, beginning with the player who has the highest-ranking exposed (face up) card. If two players have high cards of that same rank, the higher-ranking second card determines who acts first, and so on. All bets now double to $10.

13. If two or more players remain after the third round of betting, the deal continues. The dealer delivers a sixth card, face up, to each remaining player, in turn–beginning at the dealer's left.

14. There is a fourth round of betting, beginning with the player who has the highest-ranking exposed (face up) card. If two players have high cards of that same rank, the higher-ranking second card determines who acts first, and so forth. All bets remain at $10.

15. If two or more players remain after the fourth round of betting, the deal continues. The dealer delivers a seventh and final card, face down, to each remaining player, in turn–beginning at the dealer's left.

16. Players examine their secret seventh cards, and there is a fifth and final round of betting, beginning with the player who has the highest-ranking exposed (face up) card. If two players have high cards of that same rank, the higher-ranking second card determines who acts first, and so forth. All bets remain at $10.

17. If two or more players remain after the final betting round, there is a showdown to determine the winner. Players turn their three hidden (face down) cards face up on the table, and the best five-card hand chosen from each player's seven cards wins all the money in the pot. If two or more players tie with the best hands, then the pot is split equally among the winners.

18. Everyone antes for the next hand, and the process is repeated.

Simplified Seven-Card High-Low Split Procedures

Maximum number of participants: Usually 7, but sometimes 8.

Seven-card high-low split is a mixed poker game (maybe "mixed-up" poker game would be a better description). You can win half the pot by getting the best five-card traditional poker combination among your seven cards–just like in seven-card stud. Or you can win half the pot by having the *worst* possible hand, using lowball poker criteria. Well, *worst* isn't quite the right word here, because there are exceptions. Finally, you can win the whole pot by having the best high hand and the best low hand at the same time.

You can use a different combination of five cards to win high than the combination you use for low, or you can use the same five cards to win both halves of the pot.

Let's look at how we rank lowball hands...

FIVE-CARD LOW POKER HAND VALUES
(Applicable to most poker games where low hand wins)

Hands are listed in descending order from the strongest, the Bicycle, to the weakest, three through four of a kind hands.

BICYCLE (ALSO CALLED "WHEEL") *Example:* 5♣ 4♦ 3♥ 2♠ A♣
Described: A five-high "straight." (In lowball, ace is always used low.) Suits have no meaning in lowball; and flushes and straights don't count against you. Therefore, this is not a straight, but a "five high." There must be no pair.
Ties: Two or more bicycles divide the pot.

SIX-FOUR *Example:* 6♣ 4♦ 3♥ 2♠ A♣
Described: A "six high" without a five. The second-best lowball hand possible. There must be no pair.
Ties: Two or more six-fours divide the pot.

OTHER SIX *Example:* 6♣ 5♦ 3♥ 2♠ A♣ (best in category) to 6♣ 5♦ 4♥ 3♠ 2♣ (worst in category)
Described: Six is the highest rank. There must be no pair.
Ties: The lower rank of the second-highest cards wins. If the second-highest cards are the same rank, the lower rank of the third-highest cards wins, and so forth.

SEVEN *Example:* 7♣ 4♦ 3♥ 2♠ A♣ (best in category) to 7♠ 6♣ 5♦ 4♥ 3♠ (worst in category)
Described: Seven is the highest rank. There must be no pair.
Ties: The lower rank of the second-highest cards wins. If the second-highest cards are the same rank, the lower rank of the third-highest cards wins, and so forth.

EIGHT *Example:* 8♣ 4♦ 3♥ 2♠ A♣ (best in category) to 8♥ 7♠ 6♣ 5♦ 4♥ (worst in category)
Described: Eight is the highest rank. There must be no pair.
Ties: The lower rank of the second-highest cards wins. If the second-highest cards are the same rank, the lower rank of the third-highest cards wins, and so forth.

NINE *Example:* 9♣ 4♦ 3♥ 2♠ A♣ (best in category) to 9♦ 8♥ 7♠ 6♣ 5♦ (worst in category)
Described: Nine is the highest rank. There must be no pair.
Ties: The lower rank of the second-highest cards wins. If the second-highest cards are the same rank, the lower rank of the third-highest cards wins, and so forth.

TEN   *Example:* 10♣ 4♦ 3♥ 2♠ A♣ (best in category) to 10♣ 9♦ 8♥ 7♠ 6♣ (worst in category)
Described: Ten is the highest rank. There must be no pair.
Ties: The lower rank of the second-highest cards wins. If the second-highest cards are the same rank, the lower rank of the third-highest cards wins, and so forth.

JACK   *Example:* J♣ 4♦ 3♥ 2♠ A♣ (best in category) to J♠ 10♣ 9♦ 8♥ 7♠ (worst in category)
Described: Jack is the highest rank. There must be no pair.
Ties: The lower rank of the second-highest cards wins. If the second-highest cards are the same rank, the lower rank of the third-highest cards wins, and so forth.

QUEEN   *Example:* Q♣ 4♦ 3♥ 2♠ A♣ (best in category) to Q♥ J♠ 10♣ 9♦ 8♥ (worst in category)
Described: Queen is the highest rank. There must be no pair.
Ties: The lower rank of the second-highest cards wins. If the second-highest cards are the same rank, the lower rank of the third-highest cards wins, and so forth.

KING   *Example:* K♣ 4♦ 3♥ 2♠ A♣ (best in category) to K♦ Q♥ J♠ 10♣ 9♦ (worst in category)
Described: King is the highest rank. There must be no pair.
Ties: The lower rank of the second-highest cards wins. If the second-highest cards are the same rank, the lower rank of the third-highest cards wins, and so forth.

PAIR   *Example:* A♣ A♦ 4♥ 3♠ 2♣ (best in category) to K♦ K♥ Q♦ J♠ 10♣ (worst in category)
Described: Exactly one pair is present.
Ties: The lower ranking pair wins. (Aces are low.) If the pairs are the same, the lower rank of the highest non-paired cards wins. If there is still a tie, the next-highest cards are compared, and the last card, if necessary.

TWO PAIR   *Example:* 2♠ 2♥ A♣ A♦ 3♠ (best in category) to K♦ K♥ Q♦ Q♠ J♣ (worst in category)
Described: Exactly two pairs are present.
Ties: The lower ranking of the top pair wins. (Aces are low.) If the top pairs are the same, the lower rank of the secondary pairs wins. If there is still a tie, the lower-ranking non-paired card wins.

WORST HANDS   *Example:* A♣ A♦ A♥ 3♠ 2♣ to K♣ K♦ K♥ K♠ Q♣
Described: Three of a kind through four of a kind.
Ties: Worst traditional high poker hand wins, *except* aces are low.

Now let's set the procedures for high-low split. In all, if the hand doesn't terminate prematurely because a bet is uncalled, seven cards will be dealt to the players–three face down and four face up.

1. All players at your table ante by placing a mandatory token bet before receiving any cards. In our example game with $5 and $10 limits, each player antes $1. (You'll also encounter other betting limits and ante structures.)

2. The dealer shuffles. This might be a non-participating house dealer paid by a casino. In most home games, players take turns dealing, and after every hand the task passes to the left. This means you must deal when it's your turn.

3. The dealer offers the cut to a player on the right. Cards must be cut–at least five cards deep, leaving no fewer than five cards on the bottom.

4. The dealer distributes one card at a time face down to each player (self included, if participating), beginning to the left and continuing clockwise, until each participant has three cards. The first two cards dealt to each player are face down and are looked at only by the player of the hand; the third is face up.

5. The highest-ranking card among the door cards, those cards dealt face up, is forced to make a token starting bet (called the "bring in" bet) of $2. (The size of this first bring in bet may vary from game to game, and at different betting limits.) If two or more cards tie for highest rank, the "high" suit determines the player that must make the bet. Even though no suit is worth more than another in poker, for this tie-breaking, who-bets-first purpose, the highest rank is spades, followed by hearts, diamonds, and then clubs (reverse alphabetical order).

6. Beginning with the player to the left of the $2 starting bet, each player must call the previous bet, "complete" it to the first $5 level, raise it $5 if the bet is already at least $5, or throw the hand away.

7. All bets are added to the pot, along with the original antes, in the center of the table.

8. If you bet or raise and all your opponents fold, you win what's in the pot, and there is no subsequent draw or betting.

9. If two or more players remain after the first round of betting, the deal continues. The dealer delivers a fourth card, face up, to each remaining player, in turn–beginning at his left.

10. There is a second round of betting, beginning with the player who has the highest-ranking exposed (face up) card. If two players have high cards of that same rank, the higher-ranking second card determines who acts first. If *both* cards rank the same, the player nearest to the dealer's left acts first. All bets remain at the pre-established $5 limits.

11. If two or more players remain after the second round of betting, the deal continues. The dealer delivers a fifth card, face up, to each remaining player, in turn–beginning at his left.

12. There is a third round of betting, beginning with the player who has the highest-ranking exposed (face up) card. If two players have high cards of that same rank, the higher-ranking second card determines who acts first, and so on. All bets now double to $10.

13. If two or more players remain after the third round of betting, the deal continues. The dealer delivers a sixth card, face up, to each remaining player, in turn–beginning at the dealer's left.

14. There is a fourth round of betting, beginning with the player who has the highest-ranking exposed (face up) card. If two players have high cards of that same rank, the higher-ranking second card determines who acts first, and so forth. All bets remain at $10.

15. If two or more players remain after the fourth round of betting, the deal continues. The dealer delivers a seventh and final card, face down, to each remaining player, in turn–beginning at the dealer's left.

16. Players examine their secret seventh cards, and there is a fifth and final round of betting, beginning with the player who has the highest-ranking exposed (face up) card. If two players have high cards of that same rank, the higher-ranking second card determines who acts first, and so forth. All bets remain at $10.

17. If two or more players remain after the final betting round, there is a showdown to determine the winner. Players turn their three hidden (face down) cards face up on the table, and the best five-card *high* hand chosen from each player's seven cards wins half the money in the pot, and the best five-card *low* hand chosen from a player's seven cards wins the other half. The same hand can win both hands, called a **sweep** or **scoop**. If two or more players tie with the best hands, then the pot is split equally among the winners.

In the *eight-or-better* variety of high-low split, if no player shows down a qualifying eight or better for low, the highest hand wins the whole pot.

18. Everyone antes for the next hand, and the process is repeated.

Note that there is also a popular home version of seven-card high-low split, called **declare**, in which remaining players, after the fifth round of betting, declare their intentions to try for high, low, or both. This is followed by a 6th and final betting round.

Simplified Hold 'em Procedures

Maximum number of participants: Usually 10, but sometimes limited to nine. (Note: Hold 'em can theoretically be played with up to 22 players, still leaving enough cards for the "board" and for "burning." But I've never seen a game with more than 12 players.)

Hold 'em is a cerebral game, requiring both strategic and people skills. It is the form of poker traditionally used in championship competition.

In all, if the hand doesn't terminate prematurely because a bet is uncalled, seven cards will be dealt to the players, but five of them will be held in common! What does that mean? Well, in hold 'em you only get two cards for your individual hand. As in seven-card stud, you will eventually try to make your best five-card high hand from among seven cards. But in hold 'em, five of those cards are the same ones everyone else has. Those communal cards that belong in everybody's hand, are spread face up in the center of the table, and they are called the **board**.

1. There is usually no ante in hold 'em. Instead of an ante, blind bets are used to stimulate the action. A **blind bet** is a wager a player is required to put in the pot before receiving any cards. In our example game, the player immediately to the left of the dealer (or the assumed dealer position if a non-participating dealer is used), called the **little blind**, puts in a blind bet of $2 and the player two seats to the left of the dealer, called the **big blind**, puts in $5. (Other betting limits, structures and blinds may apply in different games.)

2. The dealer shuffles. This might be a non-participating house dealer paid by a casino. In most home games, players take turns dealing, and after every hand the task passes to the left. This means you must deal when it's your turn.

3. The dealer offers the cut to a player on the right. Cards must be cut–at least five cards deep, leaving no fewer than five cards on the bottom.

4. The dealer distributes one card at a time face down to each player (self included, if participating), beginning to the left and continuing clockwise, until each participant has two cards. These two cards are the only ones each player will receive during a hand of hold 'em.

5. The action begins three seats away from the dealer, with the player to the left of the "big blind" (the $5 forced bet). Each player, acting clockwise in turn, must call the previous bet, raise it $5, or throw the hand away.

6. All bets are added to the pot, along with the original blinds, in the center of the table.

7. If you bet or raise and all your opponents fold, you win what's in the pot, and there is no subsequent draw or betting.

8. If there are callers and no raise, the $5 blind (big blind) may "raise," even though he has only been called. This is called a **live blind**, meaning the big blind, being last to act, will have a chance to act.

9. If two or more players remain after the first round of betting, the deal continues. The dealer turns over three cards all at once in the center of the table. These three face-up cards are called the **flop**.

10. Players coordinate the two secret cards held in their hand with the three cards face up on the board in an attempt to mentally make a winning five-card poker hand. There is a second round of betting, beginning to the left of the dealer. All bets remain at the pre-established $5 limits.

11. If two or more players remain after the second round of betting, the deal continues. The dealer turns over a fourth communal board card in the center of the table.

12. There is a third round of betting, beginning to the left of the dealer. All bets now double to $10.

13. If two or more players remain after the third round of betting, the deal continues. The dealer delivers a fifth and final communal board card in the center of the table.

14. There is a fourth and final round of betting, beginning to the left of the dealer. All bets remain at $10.

15. If two or more players remain after the final betting round, there is a showdown to determine the winner. Players turn their two secret cards face up on the table, and the best five-card hand chosen from those two cards and the five communal board cards wins all the money in the pot. Players tied for the best hand split the pot equally.

16. The blind bets are made for the next hand, and the process is repeated.

Ace-to-Five Lowball and Omaha

There is brief mention of two other games in this book: Ace-to-five lowball, and Omaha. All you need to know about these is that ace-to-five lowball is played just like draw poker, except the low hand wins. And Omaha is just like hold 'em, previously described, except you get four private cards instead of two, and you must use *exactly* two of them in combination with *exactly* three communal board cards.

4. General Winning Advice

Here's something that confuses many players. In seven stud or many other games with early betting rounds, how should you play your strongest hand? I mean, should you come out blazing and raising–or stalling and calling? I'm sure this question has stumped humans since the beginning of time. Listen, I have the answer . . .

Magic Best-Profit Tip. Here's how to play your strongest hands on early betting rounds . . . If a raise looks natural, raise. If a call looks natural, call. Do what opponents expect.

I'm not saying you must always play according to that tip. I'm just saying, overall, that approach will make the most profit. A careful analysis of hands will show that this is the best money-making method most of the time. That doesn't mean you can't make money taking an aggressive raising approach, too. But it does mean that, on average, you'll make *more* money by playing the hand the way that seems natural to your opponents.

Let's see exactly what we're talking about here. In seven stud on the first three cards you hold . . .

Suppose that a player showing 6♣ was forced to make a token bring-in bet. Then K♥ raised and a Q♠ called. Now it's up to you. No doubt you're going to make money for your lifetime with hands like this one, no matter how you play. The question is: What strategy brings the most profit. And the answer is exactly what I've already told you. You'll make the most profit by playing the hand the way your opponents expect you to play (from what they can see). By just calling, you'll make them think you have a big buried pair, a straight or a flush try, or maybe a pair of 7s with a high kicker.

In the situation just described, it's only slightly better to call than to raise. If there were only one other active player (the raiser) and many opponents still to act, it would be even more profitable to call than raise.

Now suppose that in the situation just described you do not hold the three 7s. Instead, you hold . . .

Now what? Now, you should go ahead and reraise. Why? Because that's what your opponents would expect you to do with a pair of aces or any lesser power hand. They will even think there's a good chance you have only a speculative hand, but are reraising to establish leverage. In short, the reraise looks natural. If you raised with the seven showing, you'd be putting your opponents on alert. They'd fear three 7s, and you'd make less profit.

Be advised, you can often violate the rule shown on the blackboard. Game conditions or your specific opponents may dictate a different decision. But in the long run, and especially when you're in doubt, the rule is a powerful one for maximum profit. Finally, I want you to understand that there's really no way to argue logically that you should usually play powerful starting hands the way your opponents would expect you to . . . it just turns out that you'll make more money if you do. Next:

In the middle. When you're caught between the bettor and the player who made the last bet on the previous round, consider passing OR raising.

Being caught in the middle is no fun. Players typically call too often in this specific situation:

1. A player behind you has made a bet on the previous round.

2. An opponent called on that previous round and you overcalled.

3. On this round the opponent who is first to act, bets, leaving you to act *before* the player who initiated the betting last round.

In this specific situation, you should heavily consider passing. If your hand is strong enough to call despite this unfortunate situation, then you *can* call, but in almost all cases that you can call, you might be able to seize the initiative and keep yourself out of trouble by raising. The bottom line is, if raising is out of the question, you probably shouldn't even call.

A common mistake is to see your opponents as people of constant characteristics. Good players sometimes play poorly; and, believe it or not, bad players sometimes play quite well. It depends on their moods, and often whether they're winning or losing. So let's look at the blackboard . . .

<u>Opponents' behavior.</u> Players who just sat down and players who just got even are easier to bluff and less likely to play bad hands.

This is so important, that you should be constantly aware of whether your foes are about even. You see, when players first sit down to play poker (when they're exactly even), they've often made a commitment to themselves. The commitment goes something like this: "I know I've played bad poker in the past, but today's the day that's all going to change. Today, I'm going to sit at the table and play every hand like it matters. Today I'm never, ever going to play any hand just for the fun of it. Instead, today I'm only going to play *strategies* that make money, and I'm only going to play *hands* that make money."

People are strong. This commitment sometimes lasts half

an hour before it's forgotten in the heat and emotion of poker combat. Once I knew a player, George, who–although he almost never won–always started out playing conservative poker. Sometimes he'd get well into the second hour before saying *the hell with it* and flushing away his bankroll. George was an exception, though. Most weak players won't last nearly an hour. As an aside, and I don't know what it proves, George could also hold his breath for two and a half minutes.

It isn't just weak players starting out with a fresh stack who are more conservative than usual. Players who just got even–well, you better adjust to them, too. Often a player is stuck, buried badly, desperate to get the money back. That opponent is playing terribly. Then, pure dumb luck strikes and within a short time he counts his chips and, golly, he's even. Now, let me tell you what goes on inside a player's mind when this happens.

At that point, players make a commitment to themselves, and it goes something like this: "Well, I played like a fool and I got away with it. But now that the poker gods have forgiven me, I'm not getting into that mess again." This resolve by weak players who miraculously get even doesn't last as long as the resolve of players fresh to the game. You can figure on the just-got-even resolve to last fourteen minutes on average.

I tell this next story at half my seminars, and it's *worth* telling. It's New Year's Eve–1984, I think. I'm at the Bicycle Club in Bell Gardens, California–ten minutes from downtown Los Angeles. This was already the world's largest card casino in just its first few months of existence.

I'm playing poker that night. As midnight approaches, there are fewer and fewer tables active. People are leaving to celebrate. So, I'm forced into smaller and smaller games. It's either that, my friends, or go to a New Year's Eve party that I promised I'd "probably" attend. Fat chance! People are nuts on New

Year's Eve. Not me. I'm playing poker and so is my wife, Phyllis. At eleven, I transfer to a no-limit ace-to-five lowball game. The blinds are only $1 and $2. By all rights, this should be a very small game with pots in the $30 to $100 range.

Remember, no-limit has nothing to do with the size of a game. No-limit merely defines a style of poker. If I said, this is a *limit* poker game, you'd ask, "How big?" Same with *no-limit*. You've got to ask, "How big?" It's the amount of money that's already in the pot before the action begins that dictates the reasonable sizes of all bets that follow. Blinds of $1 and $2 in no-limit would typically mean a game in which you'd have to work all night and hold terrific cards to earn, say, $700. Not this game, not on this night. The average *pot* is more than $700, and several pass $2,000 in that hour before midnight. Remember, this is ace-to-five lowball, a draw poker variation with only *two* rounds of betting to build a pot. This game is so loose that four or five players usually stay through the first betting round and draw cards.

So, what was I saying? Oh, yeah. I'm winning proudly. This is about the easiest game to beat in America, and you could just sit there and play a whole round of eight hands for a total of $3! You could just play the nuts if you wanted to. Madness, I tell you, sheer poker madness.

Now it gets to be a couple minutes before midnight. People stand up, walk away from the table. The Bicycle Club passes out hats and noise-makers–you know, the obnoxious kind that unsnake when you aim them at someone else's face. Down to one minute. Thirty seconds. By this time I've figured out that 1985 is inevitable, so I go off to kiss Phyllis. Bingo, it happens! Just as everyone thought. Some cosmic secondhand passes midnight and everyone congratulates everyone else. Kisses, good wishes, smiles. Bullshit!

Finally, after an interminable wait, everyone sits back at the table at three minutes past midnight. And then? And then, my friends, I was playing in the tightest poker game I'd ever seen! Hardly anyone played a pot. The first ten pots were all under $50.

So, what happened? I'll tell you what happened. New Year's resolutions happened. Everybody decided to put the past behind them and play poker sensibly in 1985. That's my point. Whenever someone starts fresh, they resolve to play better, and this new determination usually lasts for at least a little while.

When opponents decide to play better, you've got to adjust. Specifically you should:

1. Pass medium-strong hands when they bet into you, because they're unlikely to be bluffing.

2. Bluff them more often, because they've consciously decided to make more laydowns.

3. Expect them to have stronger-than-typical hands when they enter pots.

4. Not *value bet* medium-strong hands as often, because they won't call with most weak hands. When I say **value betting,** I mean getting every extra penny of profit in situations where you have a slight advantage by betting.

Remember, opponents *do* play better when they first sit down and when they just get even–also after midnight on New Year's Eve, if they're sober.

Sometimes things sound so obvious that you might think they're not important. But some obvious rules are so consistently violated that it pays to stop, focus on them and make a promise to abide by them in the future.

That's why, years ago, I devoted a whole magazine column in a gaming magazine to an obvious concept I think all poker players need to remind themselves of time and time again. Here it is on the blackboard now . . .

> **<u>Caro's Law of Least Tilt.</u> Among similarly skilled opponents, the player with the most discipline is the favorite.**

The reason this is so important is that most players who develop skills at poker also acquire a bad attitude that prevents them from playing tough poker all the time. It's sort of "monkey see, monkey do." All around you are opponents who know how to play poker skillfully, and a lot of the time they do. But not always. When good players get together at the same table, a phenomenal thing sometimes happens. They take turns going on *tilt!*

You know what *going on tilt* means, right? In Las Vegas, they call it *steaming*. Maybe on Venus they call in *pressure cooking*–who knows. The point is, it all means the same thing; it means losing your discipline and letting your emotions dictate your poker decisions. If you've ever played a pinball machine, you know what tilt means. Your ball is bouncing from target to target, bells are ringing, points are jumping onto the scoreboard faster than you can keep track, you're shooting that silver sphere right back into play every time it hits your flippers. Perfect timing. And just to add to your chances you shake the pinball machine expertly from side to side to help the action go exactly the way you desire.

But if you shake a little too hard, the machine goes on tilt. The word **TILT** flashes, and the lights go out, and the flippers stop working. That's exactly what happens to poker players who go on tilt. Their lights go out, their flippers stop working, and you can see the word **TILT** flashing in their eyes. A sad,

sad thing this is, my friends. But it happens all the time.

It's become a tacit custom among skilled players to take turns going on tilt! I'm serious. Look at any game where skilled players battle each other for serious poker dollars and you're probably looking at a game where at least one player is on tilt at any specific time. They go on tilt, and they get off tilt. They play badly for a short time, then they play well awhile. Look around; you'll see that I'm telling you the truth.

When a player stops tilting and plays sensibly again, another opponent is likely to go on tilt. They take turns, you see. And this doesn't just happen among skilled players. It happens with players at all levels of play. It's just that tilt is more noticeable among strong players, because weak players don't make very good decisions even when they're not on tilt. But, I repeat: Players take turns going on tilt. And against similarly skilled players, those who spend the *least* time on tilt win the money. That's why *Caro's Law of Least Tilt* is more powerful than it seems at first.

Surprising truth. It's okay to play your best game all the time.

Most players who are capable of winning, lose anyway. That's simply because they don't play their best poker all the time. They look around them and see that no one else is playing perfectly always. And so players imitate other players, and everyone plays badly some of the time. Don't do it! Don't yield to peer pressure–it's all right to play your best game all the time.

Remember that most players take turns going on tilt. All you have to do is pass your turn. It's as easy as passing the deal.

Ego can cause us to play poorly. It can cause us to play with the intent of impressing others, rather than with the intent of making money. Ego and peer pressure, as well as impatience and frustration, can cause us to go on tilt. Additionally, ego and the silly urge to impress opponents in a poker game can cause us to make other costly mistakes. As an example, skilled players try to trick weak opponents much too often.

> **Deception.** It's often wasted on weak opponents, because the most obvious strategy is usually the most profitable.

Get it out of your head that you need to use deception against weak opponents. Careful analysis proves that the most obvious strategy will usually make the most money long term. That's because weak opponents often don't understand sophisticated strategy enough to be tricked. Do yourself a big favor: Unless you have a compelling reason to use deception, never do so against weak opponents.

> **A poker misconception.** Many players make decisions on the basis of how much they've invested in the pot.
> The truth is, money you've already invested shouldn't influence your decision at all!

Pay attention to what's on the blackboard now. Make every decision as if you have *absolutely nothing* invested in the pot. Why? Because it's the truth. You have nothing invested in the pot–ever! The pot is just a collection of money that belongs jointly to everyone who's involved. Let's say the pot is $1,000 and it costs you $100 to call. Is it worth it? It depends on the strength of your hand and the probable hands of your opponents. What you have to ask yourself is: *Should I invest $100 now in hopes of winning this pot?* That's the only question of essence. What you've already "invested" in the pot has no relevance at all.

Look, it doesn't matter whether the pot was built equally by all the players or donated as a promotion by the casino management. The pot is still the size it is, and your cards are still what they are. You don't need to know what part of the pot was "yours" to begin with. It's either going to be all yours, or it's not going to be yours at all.

> ## The anatomy of a poker hand.
> Each hand has its own attributes. One is whether it will be more profitable if played against many opponents or against few.

Do you want to play a hand against many opponents, or only against a few? Some hands play best against many foes, some play better head-to-head. Actually, I've discovered a few hands that will make maximum profit when played against *neither* a lot of opponents nor heads-up, but I'm not certain of my analysis yet, and I'll save this discussion for another time.

What you have to understand right now is that, in all forms of high-hand-wins poker, there are two types of hands that usually make more profit against a maximum number of opponents. They are:

1. Speculative hands.

2. Powerhouse hands.

By speculative hands, I mean primarily uncompleted straights and flushes. You don't have any power yet, but if you connect, you'll usually win, often beating other high-quality hands. By powerhouse hands, I mean those that you already expect to win with, even without helping.

An example of a speculative hand would be . . .

  with a flop of

This hand gives you excellent chances of winning, but you'll make more profit if you play it against a large field of opponents. The reason is that if you are fortunate enough to make your hand, especially the flush, you'll want maximum pot odds. If you raise, two things might work against you:

1. You might drive opponents out and limit the money you'll make if you connect.

2. You pay more than you would by just calling. This means your **pot odds**, the amount the pot is offering relative to the size of your immediate investment, are worse.

For both these reasons, you should automatically call with speculative hands *unless there's an overriding reason to do otherwise.*

The truth about money. Money flows clockwise around the poker table.

One concept I never tire of explaining at my seminars is how positional advantage affects the flow of money. This concept is so important that I wonder if anyone wins at poker without understanding it.

Look, everyone has a positional advantage over the players who act first. When you get to see what an opponent does before you act, you can plan your strategy accordingly. Players who act first don't have that advantage. That's why, throughout poker, players who act later have a positional advantage over those who act sooner. That positional advantage means real profit.

If you could put a weather satellite up in space and peer down at a poker table, you'd see a dominant pattern. The chips would swirl round and round the table in a clockwise direction. Sure, there would be occasional reverse currents due to one player's mastery over another, or due to sheer luck. But mostly the current would be clockwise, and it would be easy to see.

When you win at poker, where does the money come from?
Most of the money you will win at poker in your lifetime comes from your RIGHT!

Almost nothing at poker is more important than this concept. The money comes from your right. The money flows from your right to you. You act after players to your right most of the time. They are at a disadvantage. You are at an advantage. They lose to you. You win from them. Once more: Where does most of the money you win at poker come from? From your right.

Where should you sit?
Loose-but-timid players belong on your RIGHT.

Since profit comes from your right, a primary concern is to choose a seat so that players to your right provide the most profit. There is one type of player, more than any other, who accounts for that profit. The type is loose-but-timid. They make the mistake of calling too many pots, throwing money into the adventure again and again, even when their prospects are greatly unfavorable.

That's their first mistake. Then they compound this by not raising often enough when they *do* have hands with slight to moderate advantages. Thus, not only do they play too many poor-quality hands, they don't even get maximum value from high-quality hands.

Let's examine why we want these loose-but-timid players on our right. Let's suppose you're playing draw poker. You hold . . .

. . .which is a powerful hand, to say the least. Now suppose your loose-but-timid opponent has . . .

. . . which is the type of totally unprofitable hand that loose players like to gamble on too frequently. Okay. Now ask yourself this question: What would happen if the player were on my right? Well, in many cases, the player would either open the pot, or–if the pot were already opened–call for the single-unit bet.

Fine. But now imagine that the same player is *not* on your right, but rather immediately to your left. Someone opens. You raise. Now the loose player says to himself, "Hey, I'm a broad-minded fellow, and I don't hold anything against this hand. Still, you guys are asking too much if you expect me to call a *raise* when I don't have a damn thing invested yet!"

And that summarizes the problem, my friends. These loose-but-timid players typically will call the first bet with horrible hands, but not a raise if they have to come for two units and have nothing invested so far. Now, remember, you are going to maximize your profit by making a lot of raises with hands that have only a small advantage. That's the style of poker I teach, and it's the one that almost every professional player instinctively uses. Pros get the most out of their hands by often raising with small advantages.

When you raise, you'll trap the loose player with the weak hand for *two* bets if he's seated to your right. He calls (or opens), you raise, he reluctantly calls again (because he already has a bet invested and it's "half price" now). But if the pot is open and you raise, then that same player to your left will not call, period, and you'll get *zero* bets from him.

Does anyone else belong on your right? Yes. Besides, loose-but-timid players, aggressive-winning players belong on your right. That's because they interfere with your strategy when seated on your left. You want to see what they do before you commit to the pot. As much as possible, you want to end up alone in the pot against weak opponents. It's easier to ensure this if strong opponents have already thrown their hands away.

Sometimes it's hard to decide where to sit, and sometimes you don't have a choice. But always think about what seat you'd like to have–and if it can be had, take it.

> ## Take command. To maximize your profit, you must OWN your table.

Owning you table is exciting! But, before you can be excited by this concept, you've got to know what it means. That's fair. You *own your table* when almost all of your opponents are primarily concerned about what *you're* going to do next. You *own your table* when it becomes *your* stage, when opponents are confused by you and afraid to "step out of line" against you.

When you *own your table,* you change even knowledgeable opponents into meek callers who seldom raise. Remember, that's precisely the type of opponent you want to play against– one that calls with unprofitable hands, yet doesn't get maximum value out of moderately strong hands by raising.

How do you transform opponents into these meek callers? I already told you–by owning your table. Okay, so how do you go about owning your table? I teach various ways, but they all involve demonstrating confidence.

The best way I know to own your table is by using what I call the *wild image.* Before I even talk about it, though, keep in mind that the wild image isn't for everyone. Many people feel uncomfortable using it; and for some it simply backfires, because it doesn't look natural. Some other experts have written that the wild image works better in certain types of games than in others. I agree with this. Their point is that a wild image works well in a game like draw poker where you get great benefit from luring opponents into the pot with weak hands, but it can sometimes work against you in a game like hold 'em against tight opponents. In that game, you can profit from acting tight and stealing pots.

Still, a wild image can be used profitably in all games *against the right type of opponents.* Basically, the opponents should be those who call too much, or who can be manipulated into calling too much. If the chemistry of the game, the environment, and the opponents are such that you could make much money by bluffing, then the wild image may be the wrong choice. However, my experience is that almost all high-profit games are those in which opponents call too much.

Now, then, how do you establish a wild image? Sometimes I do it by raising conspicuously with hands that are normally too weak to warrant a raise. Typically, I do this during the first half hour of play. The first half hour is a very important period. This is the best time for "advertising," because it's when opponents are most likely to form an impression of you. By the way, even opponents who don't seem to be paying attention, will form an impression unconsciously. So, your super-aggressive and seemingly unprofitable play will register in their minds. The trick is to play hands in a way that looks clearly bizarre to your opponents, but–in truth–only costs you a small penalty, on average.

The hands that fit this description are simply clear calling hands. Instead of calling with them, you raise with them. Occasionally, if the chemistry is just right, I go way beyond this scheme in order to develop a wild image. In draw poker, for instance, I sometimes raise with a hopeless hand such as . . .

If the opener calls the raise and draws cards, I stand pat. I don't do this with the intention of bluffing. When the opener checks to me–which is always what happens–I simply check along. Now all eyes are focused on the pat hand I didn't bet. I spread it dramatically. Everyone puzzles over it. Why did I play the hand? Why did I raise? How come I didn't bet? Believe me, this is cheap advertising, and the result is that you'll get many more calls later when you do hold quality hands. You can even improve on this by just calling with the hopeless hand, instead of raising.

Still, that type of attention-getting play *isn't* one I'd recommend for most players. One method of establishing a dominant image that works easily against unsophisticated opponents is simply to make all your bets and raises crisp and certain. There's nothing that establishes dominance at the table quicker than making all your actions dynamic and confident. You should extend this to all your decisions. Pass with a flare that conveys certainty and confidence. Check with the same flare. When you couple this type of physical action with many raises, you'll win control of your table. You'll see. You'll own your table.

And when you do, you'll know it. Often you'll see opponents hesitate and look in *your* direction, worrying about what *you* are going to do before they act. At that point, your opponents will be meek callers. They'll be easy to manipulate, and they'll supply you with plenty of profit.

Here's another reason I favor a wild image over a conservative one for most games: *The wild image is more apt to register in opponents' minds.* When you try to bluff because you've established a solid, conservative image, you're counting on your opponents having noticed (or mistakenly concluded) that you're playing very tight. Unfortunately, most opponents don't remember your absence as well as they remember hands you were involved in.

However, over a period of time it begins to dawn on most opponents that you aren't playing many pots without solid hands. At that point, your tight image is established, and you *can* often take advantage of it.

> **Can't decide? MOST of your profit in poker comes from borderline decisions.**

I talk a lot about *borderline decisions* and *borderline situations*. What are these? They're simply times when you really can't decide one way or another. They're poker occasions when one action seems about as good as another. Most players face the "borderline" many times every hour.

Should you play a hand or throw it away? Check or bet? Raise or just call? Call or pass? It is only reasonable that many of these decisions are borderline because so often, in poker, you're dealing with plays that will only earn or lose a small percentage one way or the other.

So, you're not doing anything wrong by feeling that lots of situations are borderline. But you *are* doing something wrong if you just leave it at that. You *are* doing something wrong if you maneuver around that borderline at whim, sometimes deciding one way, sometimes deciding another.

> # Do this. When the scale SEEMS to be balanced, weigh more factors.

It's really easy to make a great portion of your poker profit from borderline decisions. That's because most decisions are balanced only on first impression. If you could weigh all the facts and think about everything you know about poker that applies to the situation, you'd usually be able to make a clear decision. Sometimes that decision (based on the *same* situation that seemed borderline at first!) will be massively profitable one way and unprofitable another.

So, what am I saying? I'm saying that most borderline decisions are not borderline if you can think about them long enough. You could make lots of money quite easily if you could call "time out" and concentrate for several hours before making a decision. Unfortunately, poker doesn't work that way. You've got to think quickly and act quickly. What's worse, no matter how quickly you think, there are always more factors you could have considered if you had more time.

But the point is this: Although you'll never be able to completely analyze a borderline decision to ensure the right answer, you *can*–at least–add one more factor. That's why I stress attacking those "tie" decisions, those borderline decisions, by considering another factor.

Sometimes, the factor I teach you to consider is a psychological one, such as whether an opponent might be intimidated into throwing a hand away now if you raise. Or the additional factor may be strategically based on other players–will they overcall if you *don't* raise and lure them in? Sometimes a tell can be the borderline breaker. Sometimes, it's the current mood of your opponent. There are hundreds of additional things you can add to break a borderline decision. You usually don't have time to think about many. But if you look to some important ones, that's usually enough to change a coin-flip, break-even decision into pure profit!

<u>**Can you play?**</u> **Whether you can play worse than "break-even" hands depends on:**
 (1) Your image
 (2) Your skill later on
 (3) Their mistakes

Classic poker theory suggests that in order to enter a pot, your hand must be better than break-even. That's obviously correct. If a hand were played in a "vacuum" with no other hands to come, with no psychological factors and everyone playing the best possible strategy, then you would only play hands that promised a profit. Hands that broke exactly even probably would be discarded, because they would add to your long-term risk without adding to your long-term expectation.

But outside the vacuum–in the real poker world–you will usually play most hands that approximately break even. For one reason, opponents are conscious of how you play and may be inclined to give you more action on future hands, even though they will likely have the worst of it. (Of course, there are rare games where you make more money by bluffing than by earning loose action from opponents, and in those games the previous comment would not apply.)

Amazingly, skilled poker players can often earn money by playing hands much *worse* than the ones that would theoretically break even in a vacuum! Why? Because, again, the real poker world is *not* a vacuum, and opponents do *not* choose their best strategies. That means that you earn money from opponents mistakes *as the hand progresses*. That's an important concept, so I'm going to repeat it. *As the hand progresses, you earn money from the mistakes of weak opponents.* All right, so it seems obvious.

But, what about this? *Because you earn more and more money as the hand progresses, you can often afford to begin with hands that are clearly unprofitable in a vacuum.*

In other words, as long as you can recoup your initial "theoretical loss," the hand is playable. On the blackboard, you saw the three main factors that help you decide whether a hand can be played. Against weak opponents whose main mistake is they play too liberally, you can enter a pot with somewhat weaker than theoretical break-even hands.

But if you've established a dominant image that causes opponents to play poorly against you, you can choose even *more* of these substandard hands and still turn them into profit as the hand progresses. The other two factors are simply how good you are and how bad your opponents are. The greater the balance of skill is in your favor, the more substandard the hands can be that you enter a pot with.

<u>False</u>–If your opponents are too tight, you should loosen up; if your opponents are too loose, you should tighten up.

The advice about playing opposite of your opponents has won worldwide acceptance, but it just isn't accurate. You should play more hands anytime your opponents stray from perfect strategy, whether they play too tight *or* too loose. The difference is that against loose players, you must bet and call more liberally with slightly weaker-than-normal hands, and against too tight players you should bluff more.

Let's take a short detour. Here's a tough concept to grasp. There *is* such a thing as a perfect strategy. It's the one you'd use in a vacuum against other opponents who are also playing a perfect strategy. But that's not the concept that's hard to grasp. The concept is that if you play this perfect strategy, you cannot lose–even if you don't adjust to your opponent's play. That means you could be totally oblivious to the fact that an opponent is *always* bluffing and you'd still win. You'd just call the same, say, 70% of the time you planned on calling when you sat at the table.

Likewise, you don't need to stop calling if your opponent never bluffs. Calling that 70% of the time will still earn you a profit. How can this be? First, consider that there's an appropriate amount of time your opponent should bluff. And he should do so totally at random. If he strays from this percentage, you can simply ignore that fact and go about your business, playing the same way you always intended to.

But, you ask, aren't you just wasting those 70% calls if the opponent never bluffs? No! First, you'll win sometimes, because your calling hand will be strong enough to beat his legitimate betting hand. Second, and more importantly, you will *never* be wrong the 30% of the time you throw away your weakest hands. So, he'll never gain anything through bluffing. Put it together and the truth is: *Anytime an opponent strays from a perfect strategy, he loses and you win, even if you don't adjust.*

That secret has led some semi-knowledgeable players to conclude that they should never vary their "perfect" strategy. But there are two reasons why they should: (1) They can make even more money by adapting; and (2) The theory doesn't always hold against more than one opponent.

The second reason is conceptually very important. Two or more players doing unreasonable things can sometimes completely defeat a perfect strategy that assumes foes are rational. For instance, if two players recklessly raise each other six times on every betting round, a perfectly programmed player, refusing to adapt, would keep sacrificing his ante and often a call or an opening bet–hand after hand. The hands he'd win would be sparse or non-existent, and his bankroll would be destroyed.

So, the theoretical argument that you don't ever have to adapt isn't necessarily true against multiple opponents. It *is* true against a single opponent–although you'll make more money if you *do* adapt.

THOUGHTS ON ADJUSTING STRATEGY

1. You never have to adjust your perfect strategy against a lone opponent; the more the opponent strays from a mirror-image of your strategy, the more money you make.

2. You can usually win more if you do adjust.

3. You probably won't need to adjust your perfect strategy against multiple opponents, either.

4. But you might need to.

5. If you do need to adjust against multiple opponents, it will almost certainly be to loosen up, not to tighten up.

6. Whether your opponents stray from perfect strategy by playing too loose or too tight, you can profit by LOOSENING UP. (Specifically, playing tighter against loose opponents is wrong, although you should bluff less often.)

7. Against too-tight opponents, generally loosen up by trying more outright bluffs.

8. Against too-loose opponents, generally loosen up by playing many more semi-strong hands (but abandon almost all bluffs).

That concludes this discussion of a very complex, misunderstood and important topic. Next time you hear the old poker axiom about playing opposite of your opponents, you won't believe it, right? On the other hand, it's not entirely wrong. And in the context that some experts have presented it, it has profit written all over it.

For instance, if you're on a limited bankroll and opponents are playing very loose, then tightening up might almost guarantee you a win. If you're playing freeze out against a single weak opponent, then tightening up could give you a better chance of winning that money (assuming there's no more to win, and nobody's going to quit until the freeze-out ends).

Lots to think about, huh?

> ## It's not enough! Good judgment alone won't beat good science.

Finally, you've probably heard many times that some players win by instinct. There was a time–a time that ended about ten years ago–when so few players understood scientific poker that the ones with good natural instinct won.

That's still true today in some small casino games and many home games. However, you need more than just good instincts to make a career out of poker now. That's because there's much new research and you face a better caliber of players today. You must learn many proven, scientifically valid concepts of poker–concepts like those in this book, and more.

5. Money Management

Nothing intrigues gamblers as much as the mystical, magical concept of money management. What is it? How can it help? The topic of money management isn't about to disappear, so we might as well deal with it.

> **Your bankroll.** In the real world you can be more reckless with a small bankroll than with a large one. Most players treat their bankrolls just the opposite.

The whole concept of money management offends me. Not that the idea is bad. Not that the term is bad. It's just that money management has come to mean something to most people that is more akin to witchcraft than to science.

Pseudo-scientists come up with pseudo-formulas for protecting a bankroll. They don't work, because they aren't borne of reason, and they can't be fitted into logical arguments. These systems just don't work, that's all there is to it.

There's J. L. Kelly's famous criterion, a mathematical formula for finding your best chance of success by considering the amount of money you have and the amount of risk. **This formula is correct beyond question**. That's because it's a rational, logical, mathematically precise strategy. The main feature of Kelly's Criterion that makes it accurate is simply that there are no unexplained conclusions.

By contrast, silly systems (those by the pseudo-scientists) often take into account the past outcomes of random events. For instance, if a roulette wheel has seen a ball land red eleven times in a row, the system might assume that black is due. Or, it might say that red is hot and you should still keep betting it. It depends on the whim of the pseudo-scientist devising the system.

Of course, the truth is that any truly random event has no ties to independent random events that already occurred. The past, in most casino games, does not influence the future.

But, I even have a problem with Kelly. Not the picky problem some people suggest–you can't easily find games where you can bet as much as you want and still divide your bets into convenient amounts to fit the formula. Forget that. The problem I see is with real life. A small bankroll may simply not be worth protecting by mathematical formula, because you can usually go somewhere beyond gambling and put together another small bankroll. Then you can try again.

I'm not saying that you can't use a mathematically correct formula to take real-world factors into account. But nobody does.

The Most Dangerous Thing I Ever Wrote
I don't regret it, but the first column I ever wrote for Gam-

bling Times magazine in 1980 was about "Plodders" versus "Adventurers." I think that column caused more confusion than any other that appeared under my by-line. The point was that it was nobody's business but your own how much of your bankroll you risked on a single wager or on a single night.

To me, back then, money management had become a detested term, misunderstood and misused. To most of those who bandied the term–the double M term–about, it meant some kind of magic salvation from losing. They thought it could help winners and losers alike. They thought it was the secret to beating casino games where the odds were fixed against them.

Money management. Their money management. It meant so much to them. It did so little. My point, in 1980, was that the more you risk, the more you stand to gain, and the more likely you are to go broke in the attempt. Whether or not the risk is worthwhile is a wholly personal decision. Only you know what the other factors in your life are.

But you must consider factors outside just your bankroll–your advantage, and the degree of risk. Those factors alone would be enough only if you played poker in a vacuum. (Yeah, I know, we're back to talking about the vacuum again.) Then, provided additionally that life were endless, you could make every decision on the basis of what you stood to gain, how much you had to wager and how big the risk.

Then–only then–the logical mathematical formula designed for the vacuum would bring you your best chance of success. But that's not how it is.

In the real world, these additional factors cloud the formula:

1. If you have only a small bankroll, it may be easy to replenish by siphoning money from somewhere (entertainment, bank account, bonus, etc.).

2. If you have a big bankroll, it's worth protecting.

3. The larger your bankroll grows, the smaller the val··

you of percentage gains. For instance, doubling a $25,000 bankroll to $50,000 will have a greater impact on your lifestyle than doubling from $100,000,000 to $200,000,000.

4. Bankrolls can be destroyed by events outside the vacuum. In other words, you could get sick and owe your bankroll to the doctor. Therefore, your bankroll cannot be wholly protected according to traditional money management formulas, simply because they don't account for interaction with the real world.

In the future, I will be releasing Caro's Modified Kelly Criterion based on these factors and others.

Anyway, back to the problem with my first column. It said that plodders felt most comfortable building bankrolls a tiny bit at a time. But "adventurers prance about the ladder of success, fearing less the sensation of a great fall than the humility of hanging idle." Unfortunately, everyone subsequently decided that there was more glamour in being an adventurer. As expected, most adventurers went broke. So, here's my updated 1991 word on the subject. Stick to sensible, mathematically proven money management (not the witchcraft kind). Be a plodder unless you're absolutely sure you will enjoy the adventure and are prepared to handle the hurt of losing.

Considering the Casino's Method of Profit. You should be more selective about which hands you play in a rake game than in a time game.

Does it matter whether the house takes a percentage of your pot, or whether you rent your seat by the hour? You bet! When a seat is rented, consider that money gone. It's the same as if you spent that money at a restaurant, or on a movie. It's gone. Just consider your bankroll shortened by the amount of rent paid. After that, you're just playing poker. So, you should make the same plays you would if there were no rent at all.

When they rake money out of your pot, that's different. Suppose you have a hand that would earn 2% if there were no rake. Not much, but still worth playing right? But what if there's a 5% rake? For this example, we'll forget about antes, and see it in a simple light. You bet $10, another player calls $10. You normally expected to make 2% on your investment of $10, so that comes to 20 cents. But wait! The club reaches in the pot and takes 5% of the $20 total. That's $1. As you can clearly see, hands with small edges are losers when the house rakes the pot. On such confrontations, everyone loses. The skilled and the unskilled.

This means you should play more conservatively in a rake game than in a rent game, assuming all other factors are the same.

> ## <u>Save your bankroll.</u> Money you don't lose is exactly the same as money you win!

Players react differently when they're behind. It's practically a universal trait. This single tendency is responsible for more bankroll failure among capable players than any other fault.

What happens psychologically is this: Players get frustrated when they fall below a comfortable loss. From that point on, adding to the loss doesn't seem like the same thing, dollar for dollar. In fact, since the sorrow of losing is already heavily felt, additional losing sometimes doesn't register at all.

When that happens, there's real danger. I call this "crossing the threshold of misery." Once you're past it and feeling sufficiently singled out and betrayed by the gods of fortune, you just quit caring. Small limit players turn $48 worth of bad cards into $90 losses. Middle-limit players stretch $680 setbacks into $1,153 losses. Top pros turn $22,000 worth of misfortune into $60,000 losses! I've seen it happen. Often. Almost everyday. All the time.

The reason it happens is that players are mentally treating a poker session as a win-or-lose proposition. That's wrong to do. They feel they have to get even or cut their losses for the night. But the right attitude is very different. The right winning attitude–the one you should always take with you to the poker table–is that you're always even when the hand begins. No matter what's happened, an expert at poker taking over your bankroll would pay for it exactly what it's worth NOW. And from the next hand on, he'd try to make correct winning decisions designed to build that bankroll.

You must, therefore, play just the way that expert would play. You really are even before every hand begins. That's an important concept, because it prevents you from squandering your bankroll in other ways, too. For instance, some players quit playing quality poker once they're winning significantly. That's because the money won is not theirs yet in their minds. So they treat it as less important. Again, if you just consider yourself exactly even when the next hand begins, you won't have the problem.

Throwing away a big share of a win is common, but not nearly as common as padding a loss through careless play.

> ## Clarification. Any $825 you DON'T LOSE is just as good as $825 you WIN!

The disaster of padding your losses can be avoided if you simply think about what's on the blackboard now. Is $825 you don't lose as good as $825 you win? The easiest way to deal with it is to play a fantasy game.

Suppose it's the end of the year and, for your records, you're tallying all your daily results. When all the $10,043 wins and the $8,455 losses, and everything else is totaled, you see that it's been a bad year.

You look over your calculations and mumble, "Gee, I lost $4,501 last year." As you sit glumly, a personal genie puffs into existence out of the fireplace. Out of the *fireplace*?! Well, it's a new variation on an old theme, so just play along.

Genie says, "How'd you like to have done $100,000 better last year?"

"That would be nice," you sigh. Then you confess, "Funny thing is, I think I made $100,000 worth of bad plays when I strayed from my game plan."

"You're probably right about that," your genie agrees. "But I can make it better. In fact, I can rearrange your life, rewrite last year's history, and make you $100,000 better off."

At this point, you notice that you've written something on

a notepad. It's your subconscious in action . . .

> ## Astonishing mathematical proof.
> $2,875 my actual loss
> -$2,050 worth of bad cards
> = $825 I could have saved

"What must I do to get this $100,000," you ask excitedly.

"Nothing much. I notice that when you added all your daily results together, you have $225,209 in wins and $229,710 in losses. Let's make it simple. In order for me to rearrange your history, I'll have to know if you want $100,000 added to your wins, or $100,000 subtracted from your losses."

"Are you nuts! What difference does it make?"

"No difference at all," your genie concedes. "Either way, you'll have $100,000 real cash in your pocket in ten seconds."

"Then take it off my losses," you decide.

"Okay," the genie says. You notice all the losing figures written on your notepad are reduced before your eyes. "Now you've got $225,209 in wins and only $129,710 in losses. Here's $100,000 in cash."

You say thanks and offer to buy dinner, but the genie becomes bored and slips back into the fireplace.

"Gosh," you mutter. "I wonder if he'll come around next year. I better not risk it. I guess I'll just have to treat every hand like I'm starting out even, instead of taking chances trying to get even for the day. The secret seems to be to make the best decision every time, no matter whether I'm winning or losing!"

Important survival warning!
Don't spend your bankroll.

Another reason skilled players put themselves out of action is this: *They spend their bankrolls.* This is a very common mistake. What happens is players seldom anticipate a long run of misfortune. But–count on this–the cards *will* turn bad for many days in a row. And you've got to plan for it.

It's a good idea to keep more bankroll in reserve than you think you'll need. Violation of this advice results in this common example . . .

A player starts with $1,000 bankroll. Gets lucky. Builds it to $27,000. Buys refrigerator, watch, 157 compact discs, a new stereo system, a wall-size TV and a motorcycle. Bankroll is still $14,000. Player now (often having promoted him- or herself to larger limits) losses $14,000. Player now broke. Player feels like loser.

Yep. Happens all the time, my friends. Now this same player, who actually won $12,000 in a short time, and who is possibly averaging $300 an hour at poker, crawls around humbly trying to borrow money to play in a small-limit game.

So, if you can avoid it, don't spend any portion of your bankroll until you've accumulated so much money that you can siphon off profit with almost no risk. Your bankroll is your equipment for doing business. It's hard to convince players that they shouldn't cannibalize their bankroll to buy groceries for their family–as an extreme example. But, in fact, winning players shouldn't. It's the same as having a print shop, and the first time you're short on cash selling off the printing press. That might fix you up in cash for a week or two, but you then have no means of survival, no way to earn an income tomorrow.

I'll say it one last time . . . please, don't spend your bank-roll.

Quitting time? Stop loss often means stop win.

One of the most consistent misconceptions about poker is that you should quit when you lose more than a pre-conceived amount of money. Poker doesn't work well with that philosophy. You see, in poker you get paid by the hour. You really do.

Sure, your results will vary from one hour to the next, but you still earn theoretically whatever your average skill merits. Therefore, if you're $60.48 an hour better than your opponents, then that's what you'll earn for each hour, on average, assuming you can play through eternity.

Some hours you'll win $1,500, some hours you'll lose $1,200, but overall you'll average $60.48 for each hour you play. You need to grow comfortable with that concept for two reasons:

1. It prevents you from forgetting that poker is your job.

2. It's true.

Because it's true, the more hours you play poker, the more money you'll win. There are times you *should* quit a game, but reaching a predetermined stop-loss usually isn't one of them.

Here are nine truly acceptable reasons why you might quit a game when you're losing:

9 ACCEPTABLE REASONS TO STOP WHEN LOSING

1. You can no longer afford the stakes.

2. You are being cheated, or suspect that you might be the target of cheating.

3. The game is no longer as good as it was originally.

4. You have reevaluated and now believe the game is worse than you had originally thought.

5. Players are inspired by your losses and are, therefore, playing better than normal.

6. You're tired or impaired.

7. You don't feel like playing.

8. There's a better game right now.

9. There's a better use of your time right now.

That's an extensive list. But there's one even better reason you might consider quitting: *You can emotionally tolerate a loss this size, but a bigger loss will psychologically damage your play in the future.*

So, you can see, I'm not telling you unconditionally to keep playing when losing. I'm just saying that, often, a so-called *stop-loss* is a bad decision. If you're winning, on average, a certain amount each hour, then quitting only means one thing–you'll lose the income that continued play would have generated.

That's so important, I'll say it again. *Since you get paid by the hour in poker, quitting costs you money.*

If the game is good, you feel like playing, and you can afford to keep playing, there's no reason to quit in deference to a magically predefined stop-loss limit. Quitting now and starting all over in the same-size game tomorrow won't protect your bankroll. You'll just lose the money you expected to earn by staying–your hourly wage. And the game may be worse when you return to it.

6. Seven-Card Stud Strategy

Here are some important seven stud concepts. By extension, a few of these can be useful in other games as well.

<u>Two cards of the same suit:</u>
Many players under-value two suited cards to start in these common situations . . .

- **When the hand is not especially strong.**
- **When there are a lot of active opponents.**

You sometimes are in a late position on the opening round of betting, and nobody else has entered the pot. Let's suppose that the lowest card was forced to make the first bet (a common method in casinos), and you have . . .

The strength of your king may prompt you to take a shot at the pot. Why? Because, (1) the forced opening bet may not call your raise and you'll immediately win the antes and the blind bet, or (2) you might stumble into a winning hand as the action progresses.

It's this second reason that makes it important that two of your three cards be suited. But that's just a trivial factor. Yes, two cards suited *do* make a difference, even one-on-one when you're primarily hoping to steal the pot early. There are times when two suited cards make a much greater difference.

First, some rough statistics. The illustrated hand (three different suits) converts to a flush a little more than 2% of the time (provided you're always stubborn enough to stay for a 7th card). Against a totally random hand, you'll win in a showdown a bit more than 47% of the time. But your flushes will account for more than 4% of your wins and about 7% of your profit. Make two cards suited, say 7♥ 9♣ K♥, and you now win more often, but only by a few percent. Flushes now account for 3% of your finishes, 6% of your wins and 10% of your profit. From these figures, it should be clear that any time it would be a close decision whether to play the unsuited hand, the two-suited hand of the same ranks *will be profitable*.

Two cards of the same suit are even more important when you unexpectedly find yourself pitted against a strong hand, such as a buried pair of aces. In that case, you won't win often, but a flush accounts for a larger portion of the times you *do* win.

The point is simple: A starting hand containing two suited cards is much better than a starting hand consisting of three different suits. Most players consider the advantage of two suited cards trivial. It is important, and with some hands it's pivotal.

Against many opponents, the suited cards are even more important, because you may need extra strength to win. With weak-ranking hands, the suited cards are especially desirable, because–just like when you're against a strong hand–a flush may make up a large portion of your wins.

If three different suits seems about break-even. Any starting hand that would be borderline with three different suits is obviously profitable with two suits.

Here we are discussing borderline hands again. Remember, when a decision seems borderline, you should search for some evidence to break the tie. An easy method with a starting hand in seven stud is to look for matching suits. If the hand would still seem borderline with three different suits, it's clearly profitable if there are two cards of the same suit.

> **<u>Two cards suited.</u> Two cards of the same suit to start in Seven-Stud don't help J♠ J♥ 7♥ as much as K♣ 10♠ J♠**

Why? A pair is not as dependent on a flush to win. Think about it.

> **<u>Big pair buried.</u> When you hold a big hidden pair and a small door card, you should usually NOT raise.**

This is a difficult point to prove, and there are situations when you will *want to raise*. But, in general, you will make more money by playing big buried pairs (i.e., those you think are better than any your opponents have) deceptively. Just call, rather than raise.

This advice is especially important in "rake" games, where the house takes a percentage of your pot. Why? One overlooked reason is that you want as much opposing money as possible. The percentage taken out is based on both your bets and your opponents' bets. So, if your $10 raise and your opponent's $10 call are taxed, the house grabs, say, 5% of the extra $20. That's $1. That means, you're raising $10 to win $9 (you get $19 back, but $10 is your bet). Clearly this means that any hand that might have earned 50¢ by raising in a tax-free home game, is now not worthy of a raise.

Let's say, instead of raising, you simply call, and another player calls behind you. Now you have $20 to gain from your $10 investment in calling. The amount taxed is $30, and 5% of that is $1.50. If you win, you'll lose just 7% of your win (on that decision), versus 10% of your win against one opponent. So, you can see, the greater the ratio of opposing money to your investment, the less burdensome the house rake will be. So, in rake games, it's obvious that you should be more cautious about raising with a big buried pair.

What isn't so obvious, but it's still true, is that you should usually just call with a big buried pair and a small ranking upcard in most seven stud situations, *whether or not there's a rake*. That doesn't mean you won't make money raising. It just means you'll make more money calling.

> **Throwing away your hand. In 7-Stud, the best times to focus on surrendering your hand are on 3rd and 5th streets (but often on 4th Street, too).**

That's just personal advice. Ignore it if you want to. But the point is, there are always too many things to consider at poker, and you'll always leave something out. Since you don't have time for a complete evaluation, the order in which you think about things is important. My advice is to ask yourself on 3rd and 5th Streets, before anything else: *Can I throw this hand away? On all other streets, first ask: How can I make the most profit by continuing to play this hand?* Of course, you then proceed to the next step of how to play on 3rd and 5th streets if you cannot profitably pass; and you think about passing on other streets if you cannot profitably continue playing.

Note that this assumes you're in a traditional limit game where the stakes double on fifth street. If this is not so, then you should probably consider first throwing the hand away on 3rd and 4th streets, instead of 3rd and 5th.

> **A Seven-Stud misconception. If an opponent plays a pair in his starting hand, two out of three times it will be of the exposed rank.**

The assumption is that if an opponent has a pair, two out of three times, it will be the same rank as the one you see exposed.

The reasoning goes like this. Suppose a pair exists in a hand, say a pair of deuces. Okay, then the deuces could fall in any of three arrangements:

1.

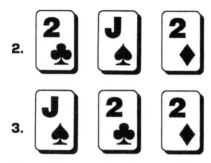

Sure, I know—there are really six arrangements, since the 2♣ and 2♦ are interchangeable. Good point! But it would amount to the same thing—two-thirds of the arrangements (four out of six) would have a pair of the exposed (card on the right) rank. You can see this easily by just asking yourself: *How many positions can the odd card (in this case, J♠) fit into.* Obviously three, and only one allows for a buried pair.

So far, this argument seems to support the contention that two out of three times, if your opponent has a pair it will be of the rank exposed. Other cards you know about clearly change the odds, but that's not what I'm talking about. Even ignoring other cards, those in your hand and ones you see around you, the argument for two out of three pairs of the exposed rank still doesn't hold.

The reason is that opponents typically show *discretion* in the pairs they play. They're much more likely to play a pair of kings than a pair of threes. If you see a king exposed and your opponent *does* have a single pair, it's more than two-out-of-three-likely that it's a pair of kings. But if it's a three exposed, it's less than two-out-of-three-likely that it's a pair of threes. That's because the opponent might not play a split pair of threes, but would *certainly* play a buried pair of aces.

In fact, there are many cases when you can virtually eliminate the chances of your opponent having a small pair the rank of the upcard. In those cases, if the opponent does have one pair, it's buried—period.

> **Intimidating with big ranks**. In Seven-Stud, when you begin with a split pair and the high card on board, you should usually make the first raise.

When you have a "scare" card exposed and a pairing card of that rank buried, the most profitable overall strategy is fairly straightforward. Raise in most home games and in casino games where you're renting your seat. Even in many rake games, it's correct to raise.

Your upcard has intimidation value. Opponents expect you to raise, and will not necessarily think a raise means a pair. From their perspective, you might have a pair or you might have something else. The reason you raise is simply that against most mixes of typical opponents you'll make more money long term. But there *are* situations in which you'll make more money by just calling. It's your choice. When in doubt with a big split pair, go with the raise.

> **Small Hopes**. You have a better chance of having your small pair stand up down the river if your opponent's hand is coordinated.

One of the great mistakes in seven stud is not calling enough at the river (7th Street). The pot is usually large enough by then, relative to the amount it costs to call, that you should usually call unless the odds against winning are extreme. Against many opponents, calling with a small pair should be almost routine when their hand looks like a try at a straight or a flush.

But sometimes an opponent's hand looks completely hopeless, like this . . .

You may need to stretch your imagination to figure out what the opponent has, and you may never figure it out. But it stands to reason it's better than a pair of sixes, because few opponents are bold enough to bluff when their hand *looks* weak. Most bluffs come when a hand looks strong, but isn't.

A bet from an uncoordinated hand almost always means at least a medium pair. You can usually lay down your hand and save the final bet.

> ## It might be more than a pair. You should usually pass with two small pair if a bigger pair bets into you.

On 4th or 5th streets when you hold two pair smaller than the exposed pair betting into you, you should usually pass.

Suppose your opponent shows . . .

against your . . .

You should usually fold if bet into! True, you might make a full house, but you probably need it even to have a chance of winning. And your full house can sometimes get clobbered by a bigger one. The fact is, if your two pair is best, it's still easy for your opponent's larger pair to improve. If your two pair is not good, you'll have trouble catching up, and you can lose some very expensive pots even when you make a full house.

Sometimes, you'll decide to call if you have an overcard larger than the opponent's exposed pair. Often, however, even that isn't enough. Be prepared to make a laydown with two small pair against a bigger exposed pair on 4th and 5th streets. You'll save money in the long run.

7. Seven-Card High-Low Split Strategy

People like seven-card high-low split because it allows them to play a lot of hands. It shouldn't allow them to do that, though. In fact, a reasonably conservative approach is almost certainly the best way to beat high-low split.

That doesn't mean you can't liberalize your choice of playable hands to take advantage of opponents who are barging into the pot with even more hands. You can do that, and you often should. Still, you need to be particularly selective about the hands you play. Once involved in a pot, the temptation to see a hand through to the final card can be great, especially since you will quite often take half the pot.

There is one concept I'll teach you right now that will permanently stop any temptation you have to play those money-losing high-low-split hands. Just look at the blackboard...

> **In high-low split half the pot is not half the profit.**

What does that mean? It means that winning the whole pot is not just twice as good as winning half the pot; it's much better than that! What? Doesn't make sense? Let me explain.

Let's suppose there are eight players and $8 in antes before the hand begins. To make it simple, we'll say only three players–you and two others–enter the pot, and all of you stay to the showdown. Let's also say that, at the showdown, each of you has invested $50, so the pot is $158 (three times $50, plus $8 in antes).

If you win half this pot, you will pull back $79, but $51 of it (your total bets plus your ante) is what you already put in. That's only a $28 gain for winning half the pot. If you win all of the pot, you will pull back $158. Since $51 of it was yours, that's a $107 gain.

So tell me: Is winning $28 half as good as winning $107? Of course not. And that's the big secret in high-low split.

Now look at the blackboard…

> # In high-low split, usually play hands that can win both ways.

We've seen how important it is to select hands that have a chance of winning the entire pot. You can only win the entire pot if you play hands that can win both ways. That's obvious, right?

In a game where there is no minimum qualification for low, the main hands that can win both ways consist of small cards that might make a straight or a flush such as…

   and

and

Of course, hands this good are fairly rare. You'll have to play other combinations, too. But keep in mind that you primarily want hands that have excellent low chances that also can *stumble into* a high hand. The exception is the pair of aces with a low card. This hand is always profitable, but is more likely to win high than low.

Even in the eight-or-better variation of high-low split, where you cannot win the low half with anything worse than an eight, you should tend to play low cards with long shot high hopes. Exceptions are if you can play heads-up (against a single opponent) or against only high exposed cards (nines through kings).

By the way, you can also win both ways if you bet and nobody calls. If everyone surrenders, you obviously win both ways by bluffing! But wait! Take a close look at *this* blackboard...

You can seldom bluff successfully in high-low split.

New players lose a lot of money trying to bluff in seven-card high-low split. There are very few situations where you can bluff successfully. That's because opponents will call and hope to win half the pot. They just get stubborn and won't throw hands away. They will hope you're going low and that their weak high hand will win, or vice versa.

If your best poker skill is your ability to bluff profitably, you may be dissatisfied with high-low split.

In the eight-or-better variety, where there is no low winner if the best low hand doesn't have an 8-high or lower, you *can* occasionally play high-only hands, but...

> # In eight-or-better, play high hands only against one or two opponents.

That's important. In eight-or-better, if nobody qualifies for low, the high hand will win it all. That means the high hand will win the half of the pot reserved for the low hand. But the greater the number of opponents, the more likely it is that someone will make a qualifying eight for low, or better. For that reason, it's usually correct to play a high hand very aggressively and try to limit the field of opponents.

When I speak about high hands, though, I'm not talking about medium strength hands you might play in seven-card stud. In high-low split, high-only hands need to be much stronger.

> ## Avoid medium-high cards.

There! Another big secret. If you've never played high-low before, there's one thing I need to warn you about. Medium ranks should be avoided. Those ranks are quite costly. Nines, tens, jacks, and even queens are almost always a sign of a hand that is unprofitable.

You should tend to play hands without these medium ranks in them. Always keep that simple standard in mind, and you'll be happy.

8. Hold 'em Strategy

Another game that helps us understand all poker games is hold 'em. I've never firmly decided what the best training game for high-powered poker concepts is, but I'd guess it's either hold 'em or draw poker. Hold 'em, of the two, requires more sophistication if you intend to win consistently.

Let's look at it now . . .

<u>Hold 'em.</u> **Abandon many straight draws against a bet if two suited cards flop. You often need a pair AND a straight draw to call.**

Once again, what I'm about to tell you is controversial. I can't prove that it's true, because I'd have to know exactly what the elements of your game are, who your opponents are and a lot more. From considerable analysis, coupling real-game observation with sophisticated computer simulation, I believe what's on the blackboard to be true in most cases.

After the flop, many–if not most–straight draws should be abandoned against a bet if two flopped cards are suited (which is most of the time). You should exclude from this advice any hands when you hold a pair in addition to your open-end straight draw.

Exceptions abound, and you must play each hand as it comes. But when in doubt, you can continue to play holding . . .

if the flop is . . .

or . . .

but not . . .

Automatic strategy. Seldom call a bet on the flop with overcards when there's a pair on the board.

When there's a pair on board and somebody's betting, it usually *means* something. Often it means three of a kind, and that's the real danger. About the best you can hope for is that opponents have pocket pairs (private hands consisting of a pair) and that your overcards will make two bigger pair if one lands on the board. You might also hope that the betting opponent has high cards, too, giving you an equal opportunity. That's unlikely. Except for occasionally trying to catch a bluff, throw away your overcards when there's a pair on the flop and somebody bets.

Essentially, this advice holds for many situations where there's no pair on the flop. Overcards are typically misplayed and cost most players money for their lifetimes.

Example of a hand you should usually pass: You hold . . .

The flop is . .

. . . and somebody bets into you. You should pass unless you have clear indications that a contrary strategy is in order.

<u>**Early position calling.**</u> **In a typical hold 'em game, it's almost always okay to just call (as an option to raising) from an early position. In a loose game or a tournament, it's usually a mistake to raise!**

For three years I've carefully considered arguments to the contrary. Many of these opposing arguments are well thought out and powerful. But, on balance, I'm forced to hold to my opinion. It is based on extensive analysis. However, be warned that my conclusion is also based on what I consider a typical hold 'em game to be. Other enlightened conclusions may be based on the assumption that a typical hold 'em game is quite different.

In discussing this particular aspect of hold 'em theory with other experts I hold in high regard, it has become clear to me that the dispute is not over logical interpretation of poker strategy. It is merely a dispute over how opponents play. I think the typical opponent is too apt to call and see the flop, and you shouldn't discourage this by raising. Additionally, I think the typical opponent wastes a lot of money by making mistakes on subsequent betting rounds, so you should welcome him into the pot.

My opinion is simply that most otherwise-skilled players are too aggressive in hold 'em before the flop, particularly from early positions. Most hands, I think, make more money if you just call the blind bets, rather than raise from an early seat. Hold 'em before the flop (and Omaha before the flop, though I'm not prepared to talk about that yet) is the only game in which I abandon my aggressive strategy for a more timid approach. That's because I feel your hand is greatly defined by three cards coming at once on the flop.

If you analyze millions of hands using a computer algorithm, as I have, you'll no doubt conclude that most of the time *you are going to be disappointed by the flop*. My general philosophy is that you should often see the flop cheaply. Then, if you have a staying hand you'll be able to outplay your opponents from that point on and win extra money. If your hand is not worth staying with, you can abandon it cheaply.

I think that in hold 'em, when you're in an early seat before the flop, there are few hands that have enough of an edge over opponents to justify a raise.

I further think that pro-level players raise too much behind a call before the flop. Again, I think they can often make more money just calling and seeing the flop cheaply. However, I concede that whenever a raise will greatly enhance your chances of either taking a pot outright *now* or ending up splitting the blinds (and / or antes) with just one other competitor, you might want to raise. I'm not saying don't raise; I'm just saying that most knowledgeable players raise too often before the flop and would make more profit if they didn't.

> **Giving up.** In hold 'em, the time to surrender is on the flop or before the flop.

Just as in seven stud, we have to decide what to consider first in hold 'em. We simply don't have enough time to take everything into consideration. The method that makes me most comfortable is to think first about whether to surrender on the flop and before the flop. After that, I think first about how I'm going to continue playing, and if all my options look bleak, I pass.

True or false. In hold 'em, if the game is very loose, it's usually profitable to play a pair of deuces from an early position.

It's true in many jackpot games where you win a special award by getting four deuces beat. But in normal games, deuces are not profitable from the first two seats. Again that's my opinion based on the way I think typical players conduct themselves.

The problem with deuces (and to a lesser extent with 3s through 5s) is that you can lose with three deuces against other small trips. That's rare, but it spells a significant net loss. If, on the other hand, you begin with 7s, you sometimes beat those same three deuces when someone else has them. It's the difference between winning this confrontation and losing it.

Another major consideration, especially against just one other opponent, is two pair. Say there's a pair of kings on board. You have kings over deuces, but might lose to kings over 7s. With the 7s, instead of the deuces, you might even edge out a player holding Q-6 (yes, they play that sometimes) if a six hits the board. But with the deuces, you lose.

What it all comes down to is that a pair of 5s is about break-even in a loose game if you open early. Therefore, bigger pairs make money and smaller pairs don't. There may be games in which *all* pairs are profitable. There may be games in which it takes a pair of 8s to have a profit expectation. But my personal guideline for a typically loose game is: I seldom open early with 2s, 3s or 4s.

> <u>**Hold 'em over-aggression**</u>**. It's usually wrong to reraise without the TOP two pair when there's a high flop.**

Suppose you hold

   before the flop.

There are a total of four players remaining for the flop, including yourself. This is the flop:

Now one player bets and another calls, and there's still one player to act behind you. Your dilemma is whether to call or raise. A large segment of sophisticated players opt to raise.

This is a tough decision, and raising is not necessarily wrong– it might solidify your positional advantage, drive the player behind you out and cause the other players to check to you on 4th Street. In spite of these incentives to raise, you usually should not. You'll make more money in the long run by just calling and letting the other player bet again on 4th Street when the limits traditionally double (at least in larger-limit casino games). If no one bets, you can then do the betting yourself.

If someone bets, you might then decide that 4th Street is a time to raise.

The problem with raising on the flop is simply that your hand is not as strong as you think it is. When you consider the legitimate betting hands an opponent might have here, about the only one you can beat is A-Q. Even that leaves your opponent with an ominous threat.

In general, when the board consists of three cards, nine and higher, you need the **top** two pair to make a power raise. You might occasionally raise for other reasons (not power), but be aware that raising is potentially dangerous. And be aware that you can usually make more money on the hand by simply calling.

Another disadvantage of raising is that you often make a bluffer abandon a hand. You'd usually prefer that the bluffer continue to bet on subsequent rounds.

> ## <u>Caution!</u> You must be very careful in selecting hands to open with from early positions.

Early positions are no place to gamble in hold 'em. The positional advantage of those who act after you is extreme. Remember, except for the blinds, anyone who acts behind you on the initial round of betting will act behind you on all subsequent rounds of betting.

It is possible that your game will be so loose, and your opponents so timid, that a hand like . . .

...is playable. But if you fear raises from aggressive players, then you won't be able to see the flop cheaply often enough. And if there aren't a large number of loose players, there may not be sufficient competition to make a speculative hand like that profitable enough when you do connect. Particularly be aware of entering pots with 2-2, 3-3 and 4-4. Also, hands like K-J and Q-J are usually not playable, although I recommend you play them once in a while for deception.

The only hands that are definitely profitable under almost all conditions from an early seat are A-A, K-K, Q-Q, A-K (suited or unsuited), and possibly J-J. A-Q suited is *not* always profitable, although you should *usually* play it.

> **Small blind action.** When the small blind re-raises an early position raiser in hold 'em, that often demonstrates great strength.

In typical hold 'em games, there's a small blind and a big blind. The small blind is usually to the left of the dealer position–the seat that would act first if there were no blinds. The big blind is the second seat to the left of the dealer, and would normally act second without blinds.

Fine. The point is that most players realize that they're vulnerable in the small blind seat. If most players pass and a late seat raises the blinds, the small blind *might* reraise in an attempt to chase the big blind out. You see that all the time, right? Some players use this tactic habitually. What you don't see very often is a small blind reraising when the opening raise came from an early position.

Most players realize, either through logic or intuition, that raises from early seats imply stronger hands than late-seat raises. Therefore, most opponents in the small blind will either pass or just call. If they just call, they get to see the flop cheaply. Many also realize, as they should, that they'll be in the worst possible betting position for the rest of the hand, having to always act first. That makes players even more likely to just call.

So, when you *do* see the small blind reraise an early position raiser, beware. Very often, that shows exceptional strength.

> **<u>Small blind defense.</u> In hold 'em, your medium-strong speculative hands should be played conservatively as the small blind when the button raises. Call instead of raise most of the time.**

Speaking of the small blind, many players have trouble deciding what to do when everyone passes to the dealer (also known as the **button**). Say you hold . . .

Now the button raises. There you are, trapped between the button and the big blind. Now what? Well, I promise that if you routinely throw away the hand, you're probably playing too tight and other players will run all over you when you're in the blinds. Raising might seem like a practical response (and in some situations it may be a good choice). But J-9 suited (along with other hands like 9-8 suited, J-10 suited or unsuited, and many more) is an example of what I call a speculative hand. It's speculative because you have little hope of having the best hand now, but with a favorable flop, you could stumble into something.

Since your hand needs to develop (especially into a straight or flush), you want to get the best pot odds you can in case your hopes materialize. By raising, you really damage your pot odds because a larger-than-necessary portion of what is contributed to the pot will be *your money*.

When you're speculating, you want the smallest possible portion of the pot to be your money. That's so important, I'll repeat it. When you're playing a speculative hand, you want as little of the pot as possible to come from you. If you keep that simple, guiding principle in mind, you'll make a lot more profit over the years.

So, the answer to this problem is to just call when the dealer position raises. The value of possibly chasing the big blind out and ending up one-on-one against the raiser is not enough to justify a reraise. Even if it works, you'll still have to continue from the poorer betting position. So–repeating–usually just call.

> **Easy bluffing. When everyone checks on the flop, then again on 4th Street, you can steal a lot of pots from the last position.**

Sure, everyone knows that. But, wait! You can steal even more pots than you think, even against fairly loose players. The main reasons this strategy works are: (1) If anyone was being deceptive and trying for a check-raise on the flop, that player will usually bet when the second chance comes on 4th Street; (2) Players are likely to surrender when they have little invested in the pot; and (3) Even if you don't win now, you might get help on the river.

In any case, players are likely to check to you on the next round, and you can often enjoy a free showdown!

> **Seeing it all. When you bet from the last position on the flop, you can often see your whole hand for free!**

I frequently make adventurous bets from last position after seeing the flop. I sometimes do this even with hands that are speculative, in seeming violation of the rule against putting unnecessary money into the pot when speculating.

Suppose I hold . . .

and the flop is . . .

Obviously, I'm basically hoping for a flush. Let's say there are two other players and they both check to me. Unless these are historically deceptive players who frequently check and then raise, I'll usually bet. Aside from the argument that I'll make the flush almost two out of five times, thus making the 2-to-1 return on my bet favorable if everything goes right and both players call, here's the real power of betting. The other players will usually check to me on 4th Street.

If I've connected with a diamond, I just go on betting as if it's the most natural thing in the world. If I miss, I just check along. That way I gain the most perfect 4th Street odds possible with a speculative hand–I don't have to invest *anything* for a shot at the entire pot!

The concept of seeing how your hand turns out for a single bet on the flop extends beyond just speculative hands. Use the strategy sparingly, but use it with mediocre hands of all kinds. If you're last to act and your opponents don't seem deceptive, bet.

9. Draw Poker Strategy

Almost everyone who plays poker, knows how to play draw. You get five cards face down; you bet; you get to replace any cards you don't like; then you bet again. This is the game where the deeds to the ranches are wagered in old-West movies. This is the game where the dance hall girl sashays across the room and stands behind the cowboy, admiring his poker hand.

You've seen this game played. You've watched the gunslingers with deep voices, snarl and bluff, while chewing on some of the most hideous-looking cigars in cinematic history. You've seen the good guys always call the bluffs; and you've seen more of those implausible straight-flush-beats-four-of-a-kind showdowns than you ever wanted to.

Even today, draw poker lives in Friday night games throughout the country. In public cardrooms and casinos, though, it has fallen temporarily from favor. That's too bad, because draw poker is one of the very best games for you to practice reading "tells" and using psychology. That's because none of your opponent's cards are exposed, and all the information *must* be gathered from body language, from what you know about opponents, from the number of cards drawn, and from the sequence of betting.

Now let's put a few of my favorite draw poker tips on the blackboard…

> # Keeping a kicker with a small pair makes more sense than keeping a kicker with a big pair.

A **kicker** is an extra card players sometimes keep in their hands when they draw to pairs. The most usual kicker is an ace. For instance, a player may start with one of these hands…

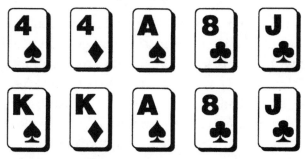

Now, listen closely. Forget the fact that you should seldom play that pair of fours. That's not what this discussion is about. Actually, in draw poker games where there is no minimum opening requirement (as there is in the common jacks-or-better-to-open variety), you can sometimes barge into the pot in late position with a small pair.

The point here is that keeping the kicker does you a lot more good with a low pair than with a high pair? You have to understand that by keeping a kicker, you're losing ground. You won't make three-of-a-kind or four-of-a-kind as often when you keep a kicker. That's because, by taking two cards instead of three, you have one less shot at catching the pair's rank.

If there's a joker added to the deck (which traditionally acts as an ace or to complete straights and flushes), you're not losing much ground by keeping an ace kicker. Since there's one extra "ace" in the deck, your prospects of improving are about the same as if you draw three. But you still have less chance of making four-of-a-kind. So, what's the advantage to keeping an ace kicker?

The advantage is that if you catch another ace, you'll have aces-up. Aces-up beats common hands like eights-up, tens-up, queens-up. If you draw three cards and make two pair, they could be fours-up, or sixes-up, or jacks-up, and those hands are more likely to lose. (Of course, you can make two small pair even if you *do* keep an ace kicker by catching, say, two sixes.)

But let's talk about what's on the blackboard. You can see the advantage of keeping an ace kicker with a small pair, but what about with a pair of kings? Well, with a pair of kings, that ace kicker is more likely to hurt you than to help you. Keeping it takes away some chance of improving to a big hand, and you don't get much in return. That's because, aces-up is often no better than kings-up. You're not covering a lot of two-pair territory by keeping the ace that a pair of kings doesn't already cover if you catch another pair.

That's why, unless you're purely interested in tricking your opponents, high-card kickers work best with small pairs.

> **Most players lose money for their lifetimes with two pair.**

Speaking of two pair, this is the most dangerous hand for beginners in draw poker, especially jacks-up and smaller. Most players, even experienced players, would make more money for their lifetimes at poker if they never played two pair! That doesn't mean *you* won't make money with two pair. It just means, you ought to know when and where to play them.

The main thing you should know is that two pair less than queens-up will usually only make money against one or two opponents. You want to avoid playing these hands against a whole herd of opponents. The more players against you, the less profitable that small or medium two pair tends to be. Often, these hands flat out lose money, so beware!

> # Open-end straights won't win any money.

You've probably heard advice against drawing to inside straights. If you asked experienced players what not to do in draw poker, you'd hear, "Don't draw to inside straights," more than anything else.

Well, that's good advice. An **inside straight** is a draw attempt where only one rank of card will make the straight. As an example, both 8-7-5-4 (needing a six) and Q-10-9-8 (needing a jack) are inside straight draws. Players look on open-end straights much more favorably. This is an **open-end straight draw**: 10-9-8-7. With that hand, either a jack or a six will complete the straight – equaling the maximum chance you can get of making a straight.

Using a standard 52-card deck, you'll only make an inside straight 8.5% of the time, and the odds are almost 11-to-1 against making it (10.75-to-1 to be exact). But with an open-end straight, you can plan on connecting 17% of the time, and the odds are slightly better than 5-to-1 against making it (4.875-to-1).

So, clearly, you should hate inside straights, and you should love open-end straights, right? No! You should hate both of them. The money in the pot is usually not enough to justify playing even an open-end straight. But the real problem is that you can make the straight and still lose to a flush. This is a disaster, because you probably lose extra bets on the final betting round that you were hoping to win extra bets on.

When you try for straights and flushes, I say you're drawing to "speculative" hands. And when we analyze the profitability of speculative hands, we discover that the second-best one figures to lose money in the long run. That means, if you're drawing to a straight or a flush, you better hope nobody's drawing to one that will beat you.

So, seldom play open-end straights. And, for the same reason, you should seldom draw to flushes, either, unless they're ace-high or king-high. The chances of making a flush (using a 52-card deck) are only slightly better than making an open-end straight. With the flush, you'll succeed a little more than 19% of the time, and the odds are 4.2-to-1 against you. But small flushes sometimes lose to bigger flushes, and that destroys bankrolls. An additional advantage of having big cards when you're drawing to a flush is that you might accidentally make a big pair and win.

10. Additional Tips

Now I'm going to put a few things on the blackboard that don't seem to fit anywhere else.

> **Ace-to-five lowball. Players who defend their blinds with low-quality hands do not belong on your left.**

I try very hard to make students know the huge benefits of choosing the correct seat. Generally, loose players belong on your right, along with sophisticated players who wager aggressively. Sometimes it's hard to choose a seat, since you sometimes have to decide between putting one or another player who fits this description on your right.

The point is, you want–as much as possible–both types to act before you. Who goes on your left. Normally, tight players who are not aggressive. They simply don't enter enough pots for you to worry about, and they don't cause you a great deal of agony even when they do.

Fine. But in games with blind bets, you often want a player sitting to your *left* who is conservative about calling bets. Why? Because you can then play very aggressively from late positions with good hopes of stealing the blinds. Or, even if you don't steal the blind because there are other players in the pot, you can sometimes make the blind forfeit that money to the pot, and then the hand becomes more profitable to fight over for you and your remaining opponents.

Some players have told me that they prefer loose players in the blinds, but that's just flat wrong! The dollar value of opponents mistakenly throwing too many hands away in the blind overwhelms the value of them mistakenly calling too much. That's true in hold 'em and other blind games.

The game that comes to mind where this can be used most consistently is ace-to-five lowball. There are fewer players at the table than there are in hold 'em and Omaha. In fact, in Omaha you seldom get a shot a stealing the blind, because opponents play too liberally. With fewer seats in ace-to-five and the table often short handed, you'll get plenty of shots at the blinds. So, it can be very profitable to put an overly tight player who doesn't defend enough blinds to your left.

Razz. In order to chase down an early-round bluff, you need a much better chance than the pot odds suggest.

In razz (seven-card lowball), one of the greatest mistakes made consistently by otherwise good players is chasing a player's bet in hopes of calling a bluff. It simply isn't a profitable overall strategy. If your hand is severely damaged on 4th or 5th Street, don't continue to call. It's easy to underestimate how much it costs to see the hand through to its conclusion. The pot odds are seldom as good as they seem.

> ## It's expensive! Don't make your prediction fit the pot.

One mistake players make once they learn about pot odds is to adjust their predictions just enough to warrant the call. Having learned the basic formula of measuring the amount of money already in the pot against the cost of their call, their brains begin to trick them.

For instance, a player will hold hands that can only win if an opponent is bluffing. Then the player will count the pot and it's, say, $140. Then he'll think, "Gee, it costs me just $20 to call, so I'm getting 7-to-1 pot odds. Now let's see, I guess the odds against this opponent bluffing are about 6-to-1. Good, since the odds against the bluff are shorter than the pot odds, Mike Caro says I get to call. Great! Here goes!" I define this as *making your prediction fit the pot*, and it's very expensive.

There are two remedies: (1) Estimate the odds against a bluff *first*, then count the pot; and (2) Put your mind in a mode where you *never* hope to call more than you hope to pass; instead, take pride in making the right decision–whatever it turns out to be.

11. Tells and Psychology

How you present yourself matters in everyday life. And it matters in poker, too. With certain images, you'll be able to bluff more. With others, you'll earn more calls. Your manner of dress, how flamboyant you are, the way you talk–it all affects the way opponents play against you.

Just knowing that your appearance and your actions affect others is not enough. You must know *how* this affects them, so you can take control of your poker destiny.

For hundreds of years, presenting a winning image at the table remained a profound poker puzzle. Intelligent players would occasionally offer their best guesses regarding the subject–guesses that were sometimes correct, sometimes far off target. Fortunately, this human aspect of poker is not nearly as mysterious as it seems.

Take a look at what's on the blackboard now . . .

Choosing the right image. The most profitable image to use at the poker table depends on
(1) Your opponents
(2) The type of game
(3) The current conditions
(4) The size of your bankroll
(5) How long you'll play
(6) Whether you're winning

What you see are some of the main considerations in choosing the right image.

If your opponents are very conservative, you'll probably want to take advantage of that flaw by choosing a less colorful image that allows you to bluff. If your opponents call too much, cash in on that mistake by making them call even more. Solid play coupled with a "wild" image works well in that case. Image will be more important against semi-knowledgeable players who can be influenced most easily by what you do. World class players tend to ignore you if they respect your play, and they randomize their decisions correctly. The weakest players think poker is bingo and don't care about you. They look at their cards and pay little attention to their environment. So, if your opponents are either very strong or very weak, you probably shouldn't go out of your way to establish an image–at least not if it means choosing costly substandard plays to make an impression.

Image is more important in games where opponents can be made to react emotionally, but not where they treat the game like bingo. For this reason, ace-to-five lowball is not a *great* game for image (although image helps). Sure, players get frustrated and go on tilt, but they also don't care who they throw their money away against. Their cards are treated like a bingo game. If they're emotionally upset and want to play substandard hands, they'll play them against practically anyone.

Draw poker, on the other hand, is a game where opponents are greatly influenced by what player they're against. So if you're image is bizarre, you can get seemingly rational draw players to call with bad hands. Image would be extremely important in hold 'em, but in many larger-limit games, the opposition is so sophisticated that they can't be easily manipulated.

Also, you should consider what's currently going on in the game. If players are about to leave, that's a silly time to waste money advertising. When you advertise, you want customers in the hours ahead, and it's a tragedy if opponents are convinced by your performance, but then leave. If there's considerable distraction at the table, such as loud conversation or exotic dancers nearby, that's probably a poor time to establish a bizarre image, because you won't get full attention.

Be warned that a loose, wild image requires a larger bankroll than a conservative image. That's because, while the image may provide more profit in the long run, in the short term you'll get more calls and end up in more borderline situations. You'll experience more up and down swings and you'll need more money for safety.

If you don't plan to keep playing long, don't advertise. You can't collect on your image if you're not in action.

Oddly, you should be much more conservative when you're losing. How come? Because opponents are inspired and think they can beat you. When that happens, many of the marginal, aggressive strategies you'd normally use to eke out extra profit backfire. Hands that would be just over the borderline on the profit side become costly. When players are inspired, they become more assertive, betting hands for value more correctly. They also become trickier. You can't count on them calling with weak hands, because they're no longer confused by your image. And they're *not* too intimidated to raise with medium-strong hands. In effect, your opponents play better against you when you're losing, and–as a consequence–you must play more conservatively.

> **Image.** **In games where your opponents' main flaw is that they call too often, a wild, intimidating and playful image is usually the most profitable.**

The most profitable type of opponent in any form of poker is one who calls too frequently but doesn't raise enough. That's a central concept of winning poker, and I'll repeat it. For maximum profit, you should always seek out opponents who call too often but seldom raise. That way they throw money your way with their weak hands, and they fail to win as much as they should with their strong hands.

Against this particular type of opponent, a wild image is usually best. You should strive to play solid poker while at the same time conveying the image of a fun-loving, crazy player who is apt to do anything at anytime. That image reinforces your opponents' mistakes. They'll call even more often; and they'll be too confused to raise and get maximum value from their hands.

> **A paradox resolved. When an IRRESISTIBLE FORCE meets an IMMOVABLE OBJECT, the immovable object gets moved around.**

The image you choose should be comfortable for you and appropriate for the situation. Additionally, your image should be commanding. You must own your table. That means that you are the one force to be reckoned with–the irresistible force. You know you've accomplished this when you see opponents glance your way before they act. This is a clear signal that they are more concerned with what you're going to do than what anybody else is going to do. That's when you own your table.

Some players will remain rock solid in the face of your seeming table command. But on an unconscious level, even these players are often influenced by you. I call these players immovable objects. Maybe in school you wrestled with that so-called classic paradox: *What happens when an irresistible force meets an immovable object?* Well, this is an historic moment, my friends. It's historic because I just solved the paradox. When you're the irresistible force in poker, expect the immovable object to get jerked around.

> **Good games.** Tables with laughter are usually the most profitable. Silence endangers your bankroll.

Additionally, you want to choose opponents who are having fun. They're less likely to treat poker as a profit-making endeavor and more likely to throw away their money during the poker adventure.

Laughter is a good indicator of a profitable table. But beware of silence.

> **Don't be fooled!** Make sure you're responding to the way your opponents play, not the way their images suggest they play.

Something I've noticed again and again is that many otherwise skilled players are harpooned by hazy images. They get a vague notion of how a person plays by listening and by watching mannerisms. This is why your image is so important–you can use it to suggest to opponents that you play in some way that you really don't, thus making them choose the wrong response.

You, too, are subject to this, so make sure you're reacting to the way opponents are playing, not the way their actions and speech suggest they're playing. Most importantly, beware of non-conformists and foreigners. Our upbringing is such that we're apt to make decisions about how opponents play from their mannerisms. Sometimes these snap judgements are right, sometimes wrong. But it's always better to ignore what those mannerisms suggest and evaluate the way opponents play by observing the actual strategy they use.

> **Reading players.** Unsophisticated opponents will usually try to trick you by acting strong when weak and weak when strong.

I devoted a whole book to the subject of tells. It's called *Mike Caro's Book of Tells–the Body Language of Poker*. There are over 170 photographs explaining when players are weak, when strong, when bluffing, when interested, when non-interested– you name it. All this is based on factual observation, and I tell you why what you see means what it does. Guesswork is pretty much excluded from the book.

The central concept in that book is that most weak and semi-sophisticated opponents act weak when they're strong and strong when they're weak. This was a concept that I and two other notable card players began exploring in detail in the mid-1960s. The other two were Art Sathmary, a brilliant and amazingly analytical world-class player who keeps notes on practically everything, and John Fox, a master of many games who later wrote the first book ever to include a detailed discussion of the weak-when-strong concept.

Why do players act the opposite of the true strength of their hands? And doesn't that make it easy to read them? You bet it does!

Even world-class poker players try to act strong when weak and weak when strong, but they do it in much subtler ways– sometimes by using "reverses" because they expect you to figure it out the opposite way–so they're much harder to read.

> **Beware!** A player looking away from you as you begin to bet is almost always more dangerous than a player looking at you.

When you see an opponent looking away, it's usually for one of two reasons: (1) The opponent has a terrible hand and isn't interested; (2) The opponent has a strong hand and is trying to *look* uninterested.

The second possibility is correct more often than you might think. So, if you're going to bet a marginally strong hand, hoping to get called from a weak hand, seldom bet when your opponent is looking away. If he's *really* not interested, he'll *really* pass, so there's no reason to bet. But if he's trying to look uninterested, he holds a strong hand and is making it comfortable for you to bet–so you definitely *shouldn't* bet your marginal hand.

> **Manner of entering chips.**
> **Players who have weak hands or are bluffing will often bet with unusual force.**

Sometimes the extra force is quite subtle. In takes a good eye and considerable training to pick up the slight tells in this category. But, in general, look for the very last split second of the betting action. If there's a little extra flair involved, it's likely the hand is weak or that there's a bluff in progress. On the other hand, if, in that last frozen instant of time, your opponent seems to take a little force off the bet, you're probably being lured into calling a strong hand.

> **Sad sounds. When you hear someone say, "I bet," with a sigh–that's a strong hand!**

Especially against weak opponents, you should listen for sad sounds. Remember, opponents are trying to trick you.

Deception is fundamental to poker, otherwise we'd play with our hands fully exposed. So, if an opponent really had a weak hand–a "sad" hand–would he go out of his way to tell you so and then bet?

No way! When you hear sighs or other sad sounds, beware! You're usually against a strong hand.

> **Pokerclack.** It's seldom loud, so listen carefully. When you hear it, almost always pass!

Do me a favor. Press your tongue against the roof of your mouth, just at the edge of your teeth. Hold it right there. Apply slight suction. Now, when I say so, move your tongue free from the suction back to it's normal position. Not yet! Keep your tongue against the top of your teeth, maintaining slight suction.

Now! Good. Did you hear that sound? Try it again. There! That's pokerclack. What does it mean? Well, put your tongue in position to try it again. Now, suppose I said to you, "I just won the lottery!" Release pokerclack now. Didn't sound right, did it. As a response to my good news, your pokerclack was out of place.

But suppose I said, "I'm feeling terrible today. My old dog Shep ran into the street and got run over." Release pokerclack now. There, that felt right, didn't it? Understand? Pokerclack is a *sad* sound.

At the poker table you'll sometimes hear pokerclack if you listen intently. You're most likely to hear it when your opponent looks at his hand or receives additional cards. It means your opponent is suddenly trying to convey sadness. When your opponent is doing that, you shouldn't be fooled–your opponent is really holding a strong hand. So, pass.

A shaking hand. When a player suddenly begins to tremble while betting during an important pot, **IT'S ALMOST NEVER A BLUFF!** Even some professional players misinterpret this tell.

When you see a player who's normally steady-handed suddenly start to shake, it usually means a monstrously strong hand! Some players, even skilled players, mistake this for nervousness and think that the player is bluffing.

That's almost never the case, because players who bluff typically become more rigid. They bolster themselves, and often they hardly breathe. Their hands are usually quite steady, almost unnaturally so.

When you see sudden trembling, it's usually a release of tension in a big pot. The player has fallen into unusually good fortune and now all that pent-up stress explodes. The result is a shaking hand.

> **Gibberish.** Any unnatural talk presented matter-of-factly indicates a probable bluff.

Sometimes opponents will try to carry on a conversation after they bet. Usually, bluffers will not. So, if you hear a player go on talking in rhythm without missing a syllable while betting, there's an excellent chance it's a legitimate bet. Conversely, players who bet and then conspicuously stop talking are more apt to be bluffing.

A really solid giveaway is when an opponent tries to keep talking naturally but the words no longer ring true. Instead of talking in a normal, intelligent way, the player is almost babbling. You can tell this is an act—an attempt to seem controlled. This is a powerful tell that the opponent really has made a weak, worrisome bet. This unnatural talk usually means a bluff. Lean toward calling.

> **Keep it a secret.** Don't act immediately after spotting a tell.

Finally, don't let your pride destroy the profit you could make from tells. Never announce that, "I knew you were bluffing," if you successfully call and win with a weak hand. Say, instead, "I don't know why I called. I almost didn't, but at the last second I decided to test you one time. I guess I got lucky."

That kind of talk will encourages an opponent to try again.

One mistake is to call too quickly (or pass too quickly) after spotting the tell. If you're 100% certain the opponent has inadvertently given away his secret hand by his mannerisms, wait. Hesitate. Then call as if unsure what to do. That method makes it less likely that your opponent will realize that a tell was involved in your decision, and makes it less likely that a correction will be made. You'll be able, therefore, to profit again from this same tell in the future. After you spot a tell, wait.

12. Tournament Advice

I decided to add this tournament section after a great self-debate. When I talk about these concepts at seminars, I usually need to explain them more fully afterward during an informal question-and-answer session. The questions always seem to be different, and sometimes it's hard to teach important keys to tournament play short of a book devoted entirely to that topic.

Here I've chosen roughly half of the major tournament concepts I teach. Some experts have done a great deal of analysis on tournament play. In particular, Mason Malmuth has written extensively (and correctly) on the subject. I've talked with top-flight researchers, players and statisticians about tournament play. I've done considerable computer analysis of my own. I'm planning to reveal the results of my studies within the next two years. One additional world-class player who has helped form my views on tournament play is twice world-champion, Doyle "Texas Dolly" Brunson. His tournament success is second to no one in America.

You should also be aware that a former world champion wrote a book on tournament poker. It's called *How to Win at Poker Tournaments*–by Tom McEvoy (along with Roy West). Many of the points set forth in that book are of great value.

> **Image.** A wild image is wrong in a percentage payoff tournament. You must master the science of inconspicuous survival.

When you're in a poker tournament, forget everything I taught you about a wild image. First of all, you aren't apt to be playing against the same opponents long enough to make advertising worthwhile. But more importantly, it's mathematically correct (once there are no remaining opportunities to rebuy) to forego small theoretical profits at high risks. If the prize money is provided on a percentage basis to the top finishers (i.e., 50% for 1st place, 30% for 2nd, 20% for third), then it's more important to survive than to get tiny extra advantages.

This means you DO play differently in a percentage payoff tournament than in a real-world game where you can keep rebuying and play as long as you please.

I'm not going to explain many tournament concepts in detail here, but I think you should have a grasp of this one. So, let's use an extreme example. Suppose you're in a tournament that pays the top two finishers—60% for first and 40% for second. Let's say there's $150,000 to be awarded, and each player (including you) has exactly $50,000.

If you win the tournament, you'll receive $90,000 (60% of $150,000); if you finish second, you'll receive $60,000 (40% of $150,000); if you finish third, you'll receive nothing.

Continuing with our extreme example, suppose each player antes $1, and it's no-limit hold 'em before the flop. You hold...

The first player now bets $49,999, going all-in, and the next player passes. It's up to you. Naturally, you're usually going to fold your two deuces, but wait! Suddenly the bettor accidentally drops his hand faceup on the table. You stare in disbelief . . .

You happen to remember that, depending on what the other player threw away, you're more than 52% likely to win this hand in a showdown. So, clearly you should call, right?

Absolutely not! The error is in thinking that if the odds were exactly even, it would just be a gamble and it wouldn't matter if you called or not. In a real-life game, assuming you have enough money, this might be true. But in a percentage-payoff tournament, it's false. Here's what would happen, mathematically, if you called with exactly an even chance of winning.

1. Before the hand started, your position was worth $50,000, not taking skill into consideration. Each of three players had $50,000, and a total of $150,000 would be awarded in prize money.

2. But if you risk all your money, double-or-nothing on a 50% chance of winning, your "share" does not get better, it get's worse! Here's why. If you could replay this situation forever, half the time you'd be out of the tournament and win nothing. The other half time, what would your position be worth? Let's see, you'd have $100,000 (actually $1 more from another player's ante, but let's not complicate this) and your only remaining opponent would have $50,000. This makes you about a 2-to-1 favorite to win the tournament, since money odds are directly related to odds of winning. This isn't quite true because real-world poker provides a slight all-in advantage to the short money. Anyway, we'll say 2-to-1.

Let's assume we play six hands total, always calling with a 50% chance of winning. If luck is fair, three times we get beat and win nothing. Of the three times we double up, two times we go on to win the tournament and claim $90,000, and once we fail to win the tournament and win $60,000 for second. So of the six outcomes:

```
3 times $0 =        $0
2 times $90,000 = $180,000
1 times $60,000 = $ 60,000
```

Add it up and you get $240,000 for six tries. Divide by six and you can see that the value of your position is $40,000 if you call. But it was $50,000 if you did *not* call!

By using an extreme example, we're able to see that when the prize money is divided among several finishers, survival is more important than extra edges. So, if a tiny edge isn't enough, how much of an edge do you need? Actually, the answer is simple. Your edge over your opponent must be big enough to overcome whatever loss you'd take if you had no edge at all. In this case, if you had no edge at all, you'd lose $10,000 in value by playing. So, you must gain $10,000 worth of theoretical profit by committing your $50,000 on the call. That means you need a 20% advantage, because $10,000 is 20% of $50,000.

Hands that would normally break even do not break even in percentage payoff tournaments. The closer you get to the prize money, the more dramatic this mathematical twist becomes, and the more willing you should be to forego small player-versus-player advantages in an effort to survive.

Also, remember that (in our example) the bettor with ace-king offsuit had an even worse situation than you did. But you still couldn't call with a pair of deuces, because the only guaranteed result would be that the opponent sitting and watching would have made money!

> **Short stacks.** You should prefer to attack short money at EVERY stage of the tournament.

Because you're trying to survive, your money is worth more on a per-chip basis when you have little of it than when you have a great deal of it. Therefore it "costs" the short stack more to call. Aside from the benefit of stealing pots from timid short stacks, a basic advantage of attacking is that–even if they don't pass–you can eliminate players from the tournament and leave less opponents contending for the prize money. This concept, and the previous one on the blackboard, only applies to tournaments in which money is being awarded to more than one finisher.

If it's winner-take-all, then each chip is equally valuable. Also, in those rare tournaments where you don't play down to the last survivor, but–rather–keep the chips in front of you when the tournament ends prematurely, each chip is equally valuable. In those two types of tournaments, you should closely mirror the strategy you would use in everyday poker.

> **Percentage payoffs.** It's usually correct to rebuy when you're out of chips.

One of the most frequent tournament questions is whether to rebuy. Personally, I'd rather not play in *any* rebuy tournaments. That's because there's no equality involved and a trophy means less. Players who can afford only one or two buy-ins are at a disadvantage. Actually, I'm not against rebuy *events*–just don't call them tournaments.

Anyway, we've got to face the world the way it is. And today most tournaments offer the chance to rebuy. So, should you? Generally, yes. Again, the key here is percentage payoffs. If it's winner-take-all or keep-your-chips, that's different. Then it doesn't much matter if you rebuy or not.

Make sure you can afford to rebuy, though. You might be able to make better use of a limited bankroll in other games outside the tournament area.

The more players who have decided not to rebuy and left the tournament, the more incentive you have to rebuy. In other words, the advantage of rebuying is greater when others fail to use it.

> **Who has the chips?** You should be even more willing to rebuy if **WEAK** players control the chips.

If the decision is difficult, look around and see who has the chips. If a large number of chips are controlled by weak players, that's an incentive to rebuy. If strong players control the chips, you may want to quit.

> **When planning to rebuy. It's best to play aggressively early in the tournament.**

We talked about survival being more important than aggressively pursuing tiny advantages on specific hands. That's often *not* true if you intend to rebuy. In fact, sometimes you should play even more aggressively than you would in a normal everyday game.

> **Rebuys not allowed. Play conservatively from the first hand.**

If there are no rebuys, survival is paramount–assuming there are percentage payoffs. You should play more conservatively than you would in a normal game. An exception may be bluffing. Often players in tournaments, especially in the beginning, are easy to bluff and you might want to increase your pot-stealing attempts.

> <u>**Bluffing.**</u> **In non-rebuy tournaments, it's easy to bluff early.**
> **In rebuy tournaments, it becomes easier to bluff once rebuy opportunities are over.**

Additionally, if there *are* rebuys, players tend to tighten up once the opportunities to rebuy end. The no-more-rebuys rule typically kicks in after an hour or two, although some tournaments allow rebuys long into the event. A few tournaments allow only one rebuy, and you should expect players to tighten up (mostly for psychological reasons) once they've rebought.

> <u>**Whom to bluff.**</u> **In rebuy tournaments, try to identify players who are nursing a single buy-in and consider bluffing them.**

If you could tell who was planning to rebuy and who wasn't, that would be an advantage, right? You'd be able to bluff the ones who were not going to rebuy.

Well, there is a way to find out. Ask them. You can sometimes say something like, "I hate rebuy tournaments. I don't even know if I'm going to rebuy." An opponent will typically tell you what they think: "Well, I'm not going to. I never buy more than once." If they say that, it's bingo! You now have valuable information that you can use against them.

> ## Hold'em tournaments = percentage payoffs. Try to see the flop cheaply.

Consistent with the concept of survival being more important than tiny advantages on a given hand, you should often forgo raising before the flop. Don't gamble. Wait to see what develops. Remember, you seldom have a big percentage edge before the flop with *any* hand in hold 'em. So, by definition, you're not sacrificing that much to wait and see what develops. I favor calling, rather than raising, before the flop. That doesn't mean never raise. It just means raise less frequently than you usually would.

> ## Players to avoid. Be conservative as you approach the final payoff slots. You should especially avoid entering pots in which players with many chips are at war.

In percentage payoff tournaments, you should be delighted to see opponents knocking each other out of competition. Unless you have an overwhelming advantage, throw your hand away and let opponents with lots of chips attack each other. It's more to your advantage to have *one opponent with $100,000* than to have two opponents with $50,000 each! That's a concept you must never forget.

Also, you should often stay out of the way and let another player who's *already in the pot* destroy a short stack. That's better than risking your chips against another well-financed player–especially if that player has more chips than you do. Two huge stacks ganging up to knock out a short stack is often mathematically disastrous. It's typically great for the short stack late in the tournament, because–although the danger of elimination is big–there's a very good chance that the short stack will move up one notch in the prize money. That will happen if the short stack survives the hand, finishing above one huge stack that was eliminated. In short, knocking short stacks out of the tournament is typically a one-person job.

Keep-your-chips tournaments. Play your best everyday strategy.

When the tournament ends at a pre-established time or when a certain number of players remain *and* you keep the chips in front of you, your best *non*-tournament strategy is effective. You simply shouldn't adjust much.

Add on? Only "add on" in a tournament if doing so will give you significantly more chips.

Some tournaments, in addition to allowing rebuys when you run out of chips, give you one last opportunity to add to your stack.

There are different rebuy rules. Sometimes you can *only* buy again for, say, the first hour, if you've lost all your chips. Some tournaments allow you to rebuy anytime you have less than a stated amount of chips left. Some let you rebuy anytime. But the add-on is different. It typically comes only once, and it is not usually governed by any rules. You either add to your chips or you don't. For instance, the buy-in may be $1,000, and for two hours you can rebuy for $1,000 more anytime you have $500 or less in front of you. At the end of two hours, no more rebuys are allowed *except* one last optional $2,000 *add-on*. That would be a typical example of how an add-on works.

While the mathematics of whether to add-on are complex and take into consideration how many players remain, the size of the prize money, the way it's distributed, the strength of your opponents, your particular table chemistry, the size of your bankroll and many other things, there's a good rule of thumb I recommend. When in doubt, exercise your right to add on *only* if it will at least triple your chips.

> ## Going all-in. Try to save your surplus money for another pot.

One terrible mistake is to lose hope and go all-in. Your last few chips are worth more than they seem to be. Mathematically, they are huge in value, especially in rebuy tournaments. There are two main reasons: (1) Short money is simply worth more, chip-for-chip (and should be protected); (2) When you go all-in, you can't be chased out of a pot, so you'll sometimes hang around to make hands you wouldn't have stayed to make if you had money.

Try to save your last chips and invest them prudently. By the way, the vast majority of tournament winners had to survive hands when they were all-in.

> ## Great tournament truth. The winner of a tournament ALWAYS got lucky.

Skill is important in tournaments. Let's say there are 300 players. That means each player, if all are equal, could expect to win one tournament in 300. If you're three times as good as other opponents, you might expect to win one tournament out of 100. Think about it. If you could win one in 100 in a field of 300, you'd really be a top-flight player.

But, you'd lose 99 times out of 100. So, what does that tell us? It shows that even highly skilled players should expect to lose tournaments unless their luck is much better than average that day.

13. Best-Tip Countdown

Now it's time for our best 15 tips of the day. I'll count them down as we work toward number one. Some tips touch on new territory. Others reinforce some of the powerful concepts we've already analyzed. I believe every tip you see is worth at least $2,500 a year to any middle-limit, serious competitor who plays poker several times a week. That's only true if you concentrate on the concepts, and if you apply them consistently.

Let's get started. Everyone should have a code of ethics in poker. How's this . . .

TIP #15

CARO'S FIRST LAW OF POKER CONDUCT. If they're helpless and they can't defend themselves, you're in the right game.

Actually, that advice is more serious than it seems. Although it's correct to occasionally hone your skills against powerful opponents, your daily profit comes from beating opponents who are weaker than yourself. Always remember to seek them out.

Tip #14

> **Calling as the big blind.** It's much more profitable to play if your call closes the action.

By closing the action, I mean that there is no possibility of further raises. Again, we're dealing with how to resolve those borderline decisions. And I'm saying that if you can't decide whether to call as the blind, then think about whether your call will close the action. If so, call. If not, pass.

Why? Because you want maximum pot odds, and any future raises will mean you have to put up more money dollar-for-dollar against the raise (or a few other callers). That extra action in itself is never as good as the odds you're already getting–the pot size weighed against the size of your call right now.

If someone raises your blind bet, and another player calls, you can close the action by calling. That's good. But if someone calls your blind bet and another player raises, then you cannot close the action by calling, because there might be a subsequent reraise. And that's bad.

Tip #13

Late Action Adjustment. Attack the blinds more liberally if they're EITHER too loose OR too tight!

If the blinds are too tight, you should bluff more from late positions. You'll win many small pots without a struggle. If the blinds are too loose, you should raise with more medium-strong hands than you normally would. That's because the blinds will then call with even weaker hands, affording you long-range profit.

Tip #12

Adjusting. Anytime opponents are either too loose or too tight, you can profit by playing more hands!

The same applies to hands in general, not just blinds. You can take advantage of opponents by bluffing if they're too tight and by betting medium-strong hands for value if they're too loose.

TIP #11

> ## Socializing at poker. Befriend players on your left. Declare war against players on your right.

Since players to your left have a positional advantage over you, you should try to make friends. That way they'll feel less like punishing you by exercising their advantage. There's no reason to befriend players to your right. Attack them strategically and keep attacking. That's where the money comes from.

TIP #10

> ## Bluffing. Seldom bluff if frequent bluffers have checked into you.

Why? Because many bluffs succeed when the hand of the bluffer and the hand of the bluffee are about equally weak. Players tend to think they always "bluffed someone out" when their attempt to steal a pot succeeds. In reality, often the passing hand was about as weak as, or weaker than, the bluffing hand! Think about it.

Now think about this. A frequent bluffer who has first chance to bet a weak hand often will. That makes it less likely, if he *does* check, that you're facing the kind of weak hand that a bluff might succeed against. More likely, you're facing a calling hand or even a raising hand that was sandbagged into you.

TIP #9

> **Value betting. Seldom make borderline bets if a frequent bluffer must act behind you.**

One of the most profitable concepts regarding borderline poker hands is this: *Consider whether the player you're about to bet into is a frequent bluffer; if the answer is yes, usually don't bet.*

You'll often make more money by checking and calling.

TIP #8

> **Adapting to your fate. You should value bet less when you're losing.**

As we've discussed, opponents are inspired by your losses. They play better and are less intimidated by you. When this happens, your marginally profitable value bets turn into losing ventures.

TIP #7

> <u>**Ego problem.**</u> **Many skilled players suffer from FPS (Fancy Play Syndrome). They'd rather impress weak opponents with unexpected plays than beat them with the obvious winning strategy. Avoid FPS.**

It's tough playing poker to impress weak opponents. There's no reason to do it, really, except to soothe our egos. In order to impress weak foes, you've got to get their attention. That means being tricky. The problem is, weak opponents are oblivious to sophisticated plays and don't really appreciate the finesses. Result? They're not impressed.

The best strategy against weak opponents is usually the most obvious one. Fancy Play Syndrome is so prevalent that I know dozens of world class players who simply cannot beat small games populated with weak opponents. Their egos won't let them win.

TIP #6

> ### Instead of calling. When you're caught between the bettor and the player who made the final wager on the previous round, consider passing OR raising.

That's important advice. Unless you can sincerely eliminate the player behind you as not being a threat, you have to hold a hand with which a raise is not out of the question to call. Sometimes, in fact, a raise may be just enough to win the pot from an opponent who, like you, also has a medium-strong calling hand but decides not to overcall.

In general, you need a stronger hand to call with in the middle position than you would in the last position if the middle position passed. There are three distinctly different strengths of hand in a three-way confrontation when the first player bets:

1. Weakest hand required to call: *Last to act after middle position passes;*

2. Next-weakest hand required to call: *Middle position after the bet with an opponent still to act behind you;*

3. Strongest hand required to call: *Middle position has already called* (meaning yours would be an *overcall*).

In short: if you'd be reluctant to call in the last position, *don't* call in the middle position; if you'd be reluctant to call in the middle position, don't overcall.

I like to think about either passing or raising in the middle position. Often, I just call. That's only *after* considering the benefits of passing or raising. If your hand is fairly weak, you're usually better off passing; and if your hand is moderately strong, you can often justify a daring raise.

TIP #5

> ## <u>It doesn't work!</u> Seldom value bet against deceptive opponents after they check.

The point is, value bets are risky business. When you bet a marginally strong hand for value, you're going after every extra penny of profit. Generally, this works best against timid players who call too much. Against deceptive players, what appears to be a profitable bet can actually be quite costly. After a tricky opponent checks, a value bet can be even worse. The opponent may raise as a bluff or, more likely, have a powerful hand which they decided to sandbag.

Tip #4

> **Sandbagging.** If you hold a "cinch" hand against two or more opponents, you should tend to sandbag if the player to your LEFT is the likely bettor.

To simplify the explanation, suppose you have an unbeatable hand and you check. The player to your left bets and the next player calls. Fine. Now you raise. Often you'll get two more calls, because players figure once they have that much invested, they're going to see it through.

Suppose the player to your left *isn't* the likely one to bet. You check your powerhouse hand. The player to your left checks also. Now the next player bets. You raise. Now the player to your left folds, rather than call the bet and the raise at once. The bettor calls.

If all goes well, in the first case–when the player to your left bets–you earn four betting units (two from each player). But in the second case–when the player to your left checks and the next player bets–you only earn two units.

By the way, if you're using sandbagging as a rare bluffing opportunity against sophisticated opponents, just the opposite is true–you'll have a better chance at success if the *last* opponent bets.

So, before check-raising a chain of players, predict which one is most likely to bet.

Tɪᴘ #3

> <u>**Why do it?**</u> **Seldom discourage a bet you intend to call with a medium-strong hand.**
>
> **Usually encourage the bet, even if you're probably going to lose!**

One common and costly poker mistake is discouraging bets and then calling. Often players will threaten to call by reaching for their chips or looking back at their hands menacingly. These actions are meant to keep an opponent from betting. They often succeed.

But hold on! When do they succeed? That's the question. It turns out that your mannerisms–designed to discourage opponents from betting–*only* work when the opponent is about to bluff or bet a weak hand. The mistake players make is discouraging bets when they hold medium-strong hands that they don't feel like calling with, but reluctantly will. It's okay to discourage a bet if you're really not going to call. If you are going to call, you should *encourage* the bet, even if you think you're probably going to lose.

That last concept is quite powerful, and I'm going to repeat it. With a medium-strong hand, you should *encourage* any bet you're planning to call, even if you think you'll lose the pot. The reason is this: By encouraging the bet, you specifically encourage bluffs. Bluffs are exactly the hands you'll beat. By discouraging the bet, you won't stop bets from hands that *beat you*–those are going to be bet no matter what. So, the only thing you accomplish by discouraging a bet when you hold a marginally strong hand is killing the profit you'd make from catching bluffs.

TIP #2

> ### Adjusting. Play tighter when you're losing.

Not only should you value bet less when you're losing, you should play tighter all around. Again, this has nothing to do with superstition. In has to do with opponents' natural tendency to play better against you when you're losing. That means many hands you could make small profits on (counting on opposing mistakes) are no longer profitable.

It's monumentally important to tighten up when you're losing.

BONUS TIP

> ### The problem with "rocks"! Tight play can succeed if used at the right time, and a tight image can sometimes be profitable. But tight play AND a tight image is usually wrong.

While a wild image is often profitable, a tight image is *sometimes* the right tool. With a tight image you can bluff more successfully. What's absolutely wrong is to play tight *and* seem tight. If you seem tight, you must take advantage of that image by occasionally stealing pots and using other deceptive tactics.

Similarly, you don't want to play wild *and* seem wild. The wild image makes opponents make mistakes by thinking you're playing much more recklessly than you actually are.

To put it simply, your manner of play should *not* be consistent with your image. If it is, you're too predictable.

TIP #1

> **The ultimate adjustment.** Here's how to play against deceptive opponents:(1) Call more often. (2) Raise less often. (3) Seldom value bet after they check.

You'd be surprised how many players fail to win simply because they don't know how to handle tricky opponents. Maybe you find yourself in a game against all weak foes, and you're winning handily. Then, suddenly, a couple strong, unconventional opponents come buy in. Now you're confused. The unexpected seems to be happening all around you and you can actually feel your bankroll shrinking.

Don't worry. All you have to do is follow the three guidelines on the blackboard. That's it. That's all there is to disarming deceptive opponents. Try it, you'll see.

14. The Great Mission

Do me a favor. Don't just think about this mission. Don't just read about it and nod your head in agreement. Instead, actually do it. You'll be glad.

> **<u>An exercise in profit!</u> How to conduct your great mission: Keep a running total of the money you've won or lost on every borderline call; keep a count of your number of calls.**

Remember, only *YOU* know what a borderline decision is. That's because, in the end, it's you who is stymied by decisions that seem to be evenly weighted between one choice and another. You're the decision maker for yourself. Decisions that seem borderline from your point of view may not seem borderline from someone else's point of view.

Resolving borderline decisions into clearly profitable choices is fundamental to my teaching of poker. But *are* your borderline decisions really borderline? Here's how to find out.

Keep two running totals in your head (or tally them on paper). One total is the number of borderline calls you make when it's the last round of betting and you're last to act. The other is how you fare overall, plus or minus. Every time you make a call that you think is about borderline (after considering everything and making your call), add one to your number of calls, and add the amount of profit to your results column if you win–or else subtract the amount of the call if you lose. Always announce to yourself that this is a borderline call before you log it. Then be sure to record the result, win or lose.

For instance:

> • 1st borderline call is $20. The pot was $220 before you called. You win. So now your borderline call count is 1, your profit is $220.
> • 2nd borderline call is $20. The pot is $110. You lose. So now your borderline call count is 2, your profit is down to $200 ($220 previous total minus $20 call).

Keep doing this for a long period of time. Try to get your borderline call count to at least 200. A count of 500 is even better, but don't be surprised if you only log one or two calls an hour, on average.

When you're done, divide your total result by the number of pre-declared borderline calls. For instance, if you made 350 calls and your result is -$3,500, then you divide 3500 by 350 and get 10. That tells you that each borderline call cost you $10, on average.

If you made 200 calls and logged +$150, then you divide 150 by 200 and get 0.75. That tells you that your average "borderline" call was worth 75¢. Finally, estimate the average amount of chips you invested each time you called. If it was $20, then your per-call result should be in the range -$2 to +$2, otherwise your judgement about what's borderline is bad, and you need to adjust. Of course, a few hundred hands may not be a large enough sample to zero in on your error. Ideally, your border-line results per hand should be no more than 10% of your aver-age calling cost, one way or the other.

If you're in a small game where about 50¢ is the cost to call, then losing four cents a pop should make you feel safe about your judgement, but winning 20¢ a call should make you reas-sess your basic poker judgement.

A perfect result is exactly even. In other words, borderline calls should be borderline. They should be *neither* profitable nor unprofitable.

This very powerful mission can help you adjust your think-ing so that you make more profitable decisions in the future.

15. Final Winning Affirmation

I conclude almost every seminar with an affirmation. I say it along with my audience. We say it loud, and we mean it. It's not done for superstitious reasons, because I don't allow my students to be superstitious.

Instead, we say the affirmation because it keeps us from doing one of the most destructive things in poker. It keeps us from destroying our bankrolls by feeling sorry for ourselves and not caring when the cards run bad.

The cards *will* run bad, you know, just as surely as they will run good. You've got to make the most from your good cards, and suffer the least from your bad cards. That's the secret of poker. But it's easy to lose confidence. Poker is lonely. Sometimes you feel you're on the world-record bad streak, and nobody else knows it. You feel like crying out and telling others about your misfortune.

But others don't care. In fact, you'll just inspire them to play better if you talk about your bad luck. So, you must never do that. And you must never convey that you're unlucky by the way you act. Instead, remember that your opponents are threatened by good luck. When they think you're lucky, they're intimidated and they play worse.

That's important, so I'll say it again. When opponents think you're lucky, they play worse. So you must always try to convince opponents that you're lucky. The best way I know to convince them is to believe it yourself.

So we say this affirmation . . .

> ## "I am a lucky player. A powerful winning force surrounds me."

. . . three times. Just when you're starting to feel pitiful at the poker table, it will automatically merge with your mind. You'll suddenly find yourself playing better, saving money, building your bankroll.

First, you've got to really say and really mean it. So, three times now, let's do it . . .

I am a lucky player. A powerful winning force surrounds me . . .

Hold it! You're not saying it, not loud enough. That "winning force," by the way, is simply the power of probability working in *your* favor. Come on, three times. It's going to work . . .

I AM A LUCKY PLAYER. A POWERFUL
WINNING FORCE SURROUNDS ME!

I AM A LUCKY PLAYER. A POWERFUL
WINNING FORCE SURROUNDS ME!

I AM A LUCKY PLAYER. A POWERFUL WINNING FORCE SURROUNDS ME!

Thank you, and go win.

GREAT CARDOZA POKER BOOKS
ADD THESE TO YOUR LIBRARY - ORDER NOW!

WINNER'S GUIDE TO TEXAS HOLD' EM POKER *by Ken Warren* -The most comprehensive book on beating hold 'em shows serious players how to play every hand from every position with every type of flop. Learn the 14 categories of starting hands, the 10 most common Hold'em tells, how to evaluate a game for profit, value of deception, art of bluffing, 8 secrets to winning, starting hand categories, position, more! Bonus: Includes detailed analysis of the top 40 hands and the most complete chapter on hold'em odds in print. Over 50,000 copies in print. 224 pages, 5 1/2 x 8 1/2, paperback, $14.95.

KEN WARREN TEACHES TEXAS HOLD 'EM *by Ken Warren* - This is a step-by-step comprehensive manual for making money at hold 'em poker. 42 powerful chapters teach you one lesson at a time. Great practical advice and concepts with examples from actual games and how to apply them to your own play. Lessons include: Starting Cards, Playing Position, Raising, Check-raising, Tells, Game/Seat Selection, Dominated Hands, Odds, much more. This book is already a huge fan favorite and best-seller! 416 pgs. $26.95

WINNER'S GUIDE TO OMAHA POKER *by Ken Warren* - In a concise and easy-to-understand style, Warren shows beginning and intermediate Omaha players how to win from the first time they play. You'll learn the rules, betting and blind structure, why to play Omaha, the advantages of Omaha over Texas Hold'em, glossary, reading the board, basic strategies, Omaha high, Omaha hi-low split 8/better, how to play draws and made hands, evaluation of starting hands, counting outs, computing pot odds, the unique characteristics of split-pot games, the best and worst Omaha hands, how to play before the flop, how to play on the flop, how to play on the turn and river and much more. 224 pgs. $19.95

POKER WISDOM OF A CHAMPION *by Doyle Brunson* -Learn what it takes to be a great poker player by climbing inside the mind of poker's most famous champion. Fascinating anecdotes and adventures from Doyle's early career playing poker in roadhouses and with other great champions are interspersed with lessons one can learn from the champion who has made more money at poker than anyone else in the history of the game. Readers learn what makes a great player tick, how he approaches the game, and receive candid, powerful advice from the legend himself. The Mad Genius of poker, Mike Caro, says, "Brunson is the greatest poker player who ever lived . This book shows why." 192 pgs. $14.95.

BOBBY BALDWIN'S WINNING POKER SECRETS *by Mike Caro with Bobby Baldwin*. New edition—now back in print! This is the fascinating account of 1978 World Champion Bobby Baldwin's early career playing poker in roadhouses and against other poker legends and his meteoric rise to the championship. It is interspersed with important lessons on what makes a great player tick and how he approaches the game. Baldwin and Mike Caro, both of whom are co-authors of the classic Doyle Brunson's Super System, cover the common mistakes average players make at seven poker variations and the dynamic winning concepts they must employ to win. Endorsed by poker legends and superstars Doyle Brunson and Amarillo Slim. 208 pages, 5 1/2 x 8 1/2, paperback, $14.95.

POKER TOURNAMENT TIPS FROM THE PROS *by Shane Smith* - Essential advice from poker theorists, authors, and tournament winners on the best strategies for winning the big prizes at low-limit re-buy tournaments. Learn the best strategies for each of the four stages of play–opening, middle, late and final–how to avoid 26 potential traps, advice on re-buys, aggressive play, clock-watching, inside moves, top 20 tips for winning tournaments, more. Advice from McEvoy, Caro, Malmuth, Ciaffone, others. 160 pages, 5 1/2 x 8 1/2, $19.95.

HOW TO WIN AT OMAHA HIGH-LOW POKER *by Mike Cappelletti* - Clearly written strategies and powerful advice shows the essential winning strategies for beating the hottest new casino poker game—Omaha high-low poker! This money-making guide includes more than sixty hard-hitting sections on Omaha. Players learn the rules of play, best starting hands, strategies for the flop, turn, and river, how to read the board for both high and low, dangerous draws, and how to beat low-limit tournaments. Includes odds charts, glossary, low-limit tips, strategic ideas. 304 pgs, $19.95.

GREAT CARDOZA POKER BOOKS
ADD THESE TO YOUR LIBRARY - ORDER NOW!

HOW TO BEAT LOW-LIMIT 7 CARD STUD POKER *by Paul Kammen* - Written for low-limit and first time players, you'll learn the different hands that can be played, the correct bets to make, and how to tailor strategies for maximum profits. Tons of information includes spread-limit and fixed-limit game, starting hands, 3rd-7th street strategy, overcards, psychology and much more. 192 pgs. $14.95.

OMAHA HI-LO POKER *by Shane Smith* - Learn essential winning strategies for beating Omaha high-low; the best starting hands, how to play the flop, turn, and river, how to read the board for both high and low, dangerous draws, and how to win low-limit tournaments. Smith shows the differences between Omaha high-low and hold'em strategies. Includes odds charts, glossary, low-limit tips, strategic ideas. 84 pages, 8 x 11, spiral bound, $17.95.

7-CARD STUD (THE COMPLETE COURSE IN WINNING AT MEDIUM & LOWER LIMITS) *by Roy West* - Learn the latest strategies for winning at $1-$4 spread-limit up to $10-$20 fixed-limit games. Covers starting hands, 3rd-7th street strategy for playing most hands, overcards, selective aggressiveness, reading hands, secrets of the pros, psychology, more in a 42 lesson informal format. Includes bonus chapter on 7-stud tournament strategy by World Champion Tom McEvoy. 160 pages, paperback, $24.95.

WINNING LOW LIMIT HOLD'EM *by Lee Jones* - This essential book on playing 1-4, 3-6, and 1-4-8-8 low limit hold'em is packed with insights on winning: pre-flop positional play; playing the flop in all positions with a pair, two pair, trips, overcards, draws, made and nothing hands; turn and river play; how to read the board; avoiding trash hands; using the check-raise; bluffing, stereotypes, much more. Includes quizzes with answers. Terrific book. 176 pages, 5 1/2 x 8 1/2, paperback, $19.95.

BIG BOOK OF POKER *by Ken Warren* - This easy-to-read and oversized guide teaches you everything you need to know to win money at home poker, and in cardrooms, casinos and on the tournament circuit. Readers will learn how to bet, raise, and checkraise, bluff, semi-bluff, and how to take advantage of position and pot odds. Great sections on hold'em (plus, stud games, Omaha, draw games, and many more) and playing and winning poker on the internet. Packed with charts, diagrams, sidebars, and detailed, easy-to-read examples by best-selling poker expert Ken Warren, this wonderfully formatted book is one stop shopping for players ready to take on any form of poker for real money. Want to be a big player? Buy the Big Book of Poker! 336 oversized pgs, $19.95.

WINNING POKER FOR THE SERIOUS PLAYER *by Edwin Silberstang* - More than 100 actual examples and tons of advice on beating 7 Card Stud, Texas Hold 'Em, Draw Poker, Loball, High-Low and 10 other variations. Silberstang analyzes the essentials of being a great player; reading tells, analyzing tables, playing position, mastering the art of deception, creating fear at the table. Also, psychological tactics, when to play aggressive or slow play, or fold, expert plays, more. Colorful glossary included. 304 pages, 6 x 9, $16.95.

HOW TO PLAY WINNING POKER *by Avery Cardoza* - New and expanded edition shows playing and winning strategies for all major games: five & seven stud games, Omaha, draw poker, hold'em, and high-low, both for home and casino play. You'll learn 15 winning poker concepts, how to minimize losses and maximize profits, how to read opponents and gain the edge against their style, how to use use pot odds, tells, position, more. 160 pgs. $12.95

Order Toll-Free 1-800-577-WINS or use order form on page 159

We have new poker books coming out all the time.
To see our full range of poker titles, visit our web site:

www.cardozapub.com

FROM CARDSMITH'S EXCITING LIBRARY
ADD THESE TO YOUR COLLECTION - ORDER NOW!

NO-LIMIT TEXAS HOLD 'EM: The New Player's Guide to Winning Poker's Biggest Game *by Brad Daugherty & Tom McEvoy.* For experienced limit players who want to play no-limit or rookies who has never played before, two world champions give readers a crash course in how to join the elite ranks of million-dollar, no-limit hold'em tournament winners and cash game players. Readers learn the winning principles and four major skills: how to evaluate the strength of a hand, determine how much to bet, how to understand opponents' play, and how to bluff and when to do it. 74 game scenarios, two unique betting charts for tournament play and sections on essential principles and strategies, show you how to get to the winners' circle. Special section on beating online tournaments. 288 pages, $24.95.

COWBOYS, GAMBLERS & HUSTLERS: The True Adventures of a Rodeo Champion & Poker Legend by *Byron "Cowboy" Wolford.* Ride along with the road gamblers as they fade the white line from Dallas to Shreveport to Houston in the 1960s in search of a score. Feel the fear and frustration of being hijacked, getting arrested for playing poker, and having to outwit card sharps and scam artists. Wolford survived it all to win a WSOP gold bracelet playing with poker greats Amarillo Slim Preston, Johnny Moss and Bobby Baldwin (and 30 rodeo belt buckles). Read fascinating yarns about life on the rough and tumble, and colorful adventures as a road gambler and hustler gambling in smoky backrooms with legends Titanic Thompson, Jack Straus, Doyle Brunson and get a look at vintage Las Vegas when Cowboy's friend, Benny Binion ruled Glitter Gulch. Read about the most famous bluff in WSOP history. Endorsed by Jack Binion, Doyle Brunson & Bobby Baldwin, who says, *Cowboy is probably the best gambling story teller in the world.* 304 pages, $19.95.

SECRETS OF WINNING POKER by *Tex Sheahan.* This is a compilation of Sheahan's best articles from 15 years of writing for the major gaming magazines as his legacy to poker players. Sheahan gives you sound advice on winning poker strategies for hold'em and 7-card stud. Chapters on tournament play, psychology, personality profiles and some very funny stories from the greenfelt jungle. "Some of the best advice you'll ever read on how to win at poker" -- Doyle Brunson. 200 pages, paperback. Originally $19.95, now only $14.95.

OMAHA HI-LO: Play to Win with the Odds by *Bill Boston.* Selecting the right hands to play is the most important decision you'll make in Omaha high-low poker. In this book you'll find the odds for every hand dealt in Omaha high-low—the chances that the hand has of winning the high end of the pot, the low end of it, and how often it is expected to scoop the whole pot. The results are based on 10,000 simulations for each one of the possible 5,211 Omaha high-low hands. Boston has organized the data into an easy-to-use format and added insights learned from years of experience. Learn the 5,211 Omaha high-low hands, the 49 best hands and their odds, the 49 worst hands, trap hands to avoid, and 30 Ace-less hands you can play for profit. A great tool for Omaha players! 156 pages, $19.95.

OMAHA HI-LO POKER (8 OR BETTER): How to win at the lower limits by *Shane Smith.* Since its first printing in 1991, this has become the classic in the field for low-limit players. Readers have lauded the author's clear and concise writing style. Smith shows you how to put players on hands, read the board for high and low, avoid dangerous draws, and use winning betting strategies. Chapters include starting hands, the flop, the turn, the river, and tournament strategy. Illustrated with pictorials of sample hands, an odds chart, and a starting hands chart. Lou Krieger, author of *Poker for Dummies,* says, *Shane Smith's book is terrific! If you're new to Omaha high-low split or if you're a low-limit player who wants to improve your game, you ought to have this book in your poker library. Complex concepts are presented in an easy-to-understand format. It's a gem!* 82 pages, spiralbound. $17.95.

THE WACKY SIDE OF POKER by *Ralph E. Wheeler.* Take a walk on the wacky side with 88 humorous poker cartoons! Also includes 220 wise and witty poker quotes. Lighten up from all the heavy reading and preparation of the games wit a quick walk through this fun book. Perfect for holiday gifting. 176 pages filled with wit and wisdom will bring a smile to your face. At less than a ten-spot, you can't go wrong! 176 pages, $9.95.

THE CHAMPIONSHIP SERIES
POWERFUL BOOKS YOU <u>MUST</u> HAVE

CHAMPIONSHIP TOURNAMENT POKER by *Tom McEvoy*. New Cardoza Edition! Rated by pros as best book on tournaments ever written and enthusiastically endorsed by more than 5 world champions, this is the definitive guide to winning tournaments and a *must* for every player's library. McEvoy lets you in on the secrets he has used to win millions of dollars in tournaments and the insights he has learned competing against the best players in the world. Packed solid with winning strategies for all 11 games in the *World Series of Poker*, with extensive discussions of 7-card stud, limit hold'em, pot and no-limit hold'em, Omaha high-low, re-buy, half-half tournaments, satellites, strategies for each stage of tournaments. Tons of essential concepts and specific strategies jam-pack the book. Phil Hellmuth, 1989 WSOP champion says, *[this] is the world's most definitive guide to winning poker tournaments*. 416 pages, paperback, $29.95.

CHAMPIONSHIP TABLE (at the World Series of Poker) by *Dana Smith, Ralph Wheeler, and Tom McEvoy*. New Cardoza Edition! From 1970 when the champion was presented a silver cup, to the present when the champion was awarded more than $2 million, Championship Table celebrates three decades of poker greats who have competed to win poker's most coveted title. This book gives you the names and photographs of all the players who made the final table, pictures the last hand the champion played against the runner-up, how they played their cards, and how much they won. There is also features fascinating interviews and conversations with the champions and runners-up and interesting highlights from each Series. This is a fascinating and invaluable resource book for WSOP and gaming buffs. In some cases the champion himself wrote "how it happened," as did two-time champion Doyle Brunson when Stu Ungar caught a wheel in 1980 on the turn to deprive "Texas Dolly" of his third title. Includes tons of vintage photographs. 208 pages, paperback, $19.95.

CHAMPIONSHIP SATELLITE STRATEGY by *Brad Dougherty & Tom McEvoy*. In 2002 and 2003 satellite players won their way into the $10,000 WSOP buy-in and emerged as champions, winning more than $2 million each. You can too! You'll learn specific, proven strategies for winning almost any satellite. Learn the 10 ways to win a seat at the WSOP and other big tournaments, how to win limit hold'em and no-limit hold'em satellites, one-table satellites for big tournaments, and online satellites, plus how to play the final table of super satellites. McEvoy and Daugherty sincerely believe that if you practice these strategies, you can win your way into any tournament for a fraction of the buy-in. You'll learn how much to bet, how hard to pressure opponents, how to tell when an opponent is bluffing, how to play deceptively, and how to use your chips as weapons of destruction. Includes a special chapter on no-limit hold'em satellites! 256 pages. illustrated hands, photos, glossary. $24.95.

CHAMPIONSHIP PRACTICE HANDS by *T. J. Cloutier & Tom McEvoy*. Two tournament legends show you how to become a winning tournament player. Get inside their heads as they think they way through the correct strategy at 57 limit and no-limit practice hands. Cloutier & McEvoy show you how to use your skill and intuition to play strategic hands for maximum profit in real tournament scenarios and how 45 key hands were played by champions in turnaround situations at the WSOP. By sharing their analysis on how the winners and losers played key hands, you'll gain tremendous insights into how tournament poker is played at the highest levels. Learn how champions think and how they play major hands in strategic tournament situations, Cloutier and McEvoy believe that you will be able to win your share of the profits in today's tournaments -- and join them at the championship table far sooner than you ever imagined. 288 pages, illustrated with card pictures, $29.95

THE CHAMPIONSHIP SERIES
POWERFUL BOOKS YOU <u>MUST</u> HAVE

CHAMPIONSHIP HOLD'EM *by T. J. Cloutier & Tom McEvoy.* Hard-hitting hold'em the way it's played *today* in both limit cash games and tournaments. Get killer advice on how to win more money in rammin'-jammin' games, kill-pot, jackpot, shorthanded, and other types of cash games. You'll learn the thinking process before the flop, on the flop, on the turn, and at the river with specific suggestions for what to do when good or bad things happen plus 20 illustrated hands with play-by-play analyses. Specific advice for rocks in tight games, weaklings in loose games, experts in solid games, how hand values change in jackpot games, when you should fold, check, raise, reraise, check-raise, slowplay, bluff, and tournament strategies for small buy-in, big buy-in, rebuy, incremental add-on, satellite and big-field major tournaments. Wow! Easy-to-read and conversational, if you want to become a lifelong winner at limit hold'em, you need this book! 320 Pages, Illustrated, Photos. $39.95

CHAMPIONSHIP NO-LIMIT & POT-LIMIT HOLD'EM *by T. J. Cloutier & Tom McEvoy* New Cardoza edition! This is the bible of winning pot-limit and no-limit hold'em tournaments, the definitive guide to winning at two of the world's most exciting poker games! Written by eight-time World Champion players T.J. Cloutier (1998 *and* 2002 Player of the Year) and Tom McEvoy (the foremost author on tournament strategy) who have won millions of dollars each playing no-limit and pot-limit hold'em in cash games and major tournaments around the world. You'll get all the answers here —no holds barred—to your most important questions: How do you get inside your opponents' heads and learn how to beat them at their own game? How can you tell how much to bet, raise, and reraise in no-limit hold'em? When can you bluff? How do you set up your opponents in pot-limit hold'em so that you can win a monster pot? What are the best strategies for winning no-limit and pot-limit tournaments, satellites, and supersatellites? Rock-solid and inspired advice from two of the most recognizable figures in poker — advice that you can bank on. If you want to become a future champion, you must have this book. 304 pages, paperback, photos. $29.95

CHAMPIONSHIP OMAHA (Omaha High-Low, Pot-limit Omaha, Limit High Omaha) *by T. J. Cloutier & Tom McEvoy.* Clearly-written strategies and powerful advice from Cloutier and McEvoy who have won four World Series of Poker titles in Omaha tournaments. Powerful advice shows you how to win at low-limit and high-stakes games, how to play against loose and tight opponents, and the differing strategies for rebuy and freezeout tournaments. Learn the best starting hands, when slowplaying a big hand is dangerous, what danglers are and why winners don't play them, why pot-limit Omaha is the only poker game where you sometimes fold the nuts on the flop and are correct in doing so and overall, how can you win a lot of money at Omaha! 230 pages, photos, illustrations, $39.95.

CHAMPIONSHIP STUD (Seven-Card Stud, Stud 8/or Better and Razz) *by Dr. Max Stern, Linda Johnson, and Tom McEvoy.* The authors, who have earned millions of dollars in major tournaments and cash games, eight World Series of Poker bracelets and hundreds of other titles in competition against the best players in the world show you the winning strategies for medium-limit side games as well as poker tournaments and a general tournament strategy that is applicable to any form of poker. Includes give-and-take conversations between the authors to give you more than one point of view on how to play poker. 200 pages, hand pictorials, photos. $29.95.

Order Toll-Free 1-800-577-WINS or use order form on page 159

VIDEOS BY MIKE CARO
THE MAD GENIUS OF POKER

CARO'S PRO POKER TELLS

The long-awaited two-video set is a powerful scientific course on how to use your opponents' gestures, words and body language to read their hands and win all their money. These carefully guarded poker secrets, filmed with 63 poker notables, will revolutionize your game. It reveals when opponents are bluffing, when they aren't, and why. Knowing what your opponent's gestures mean, and protecting them from knowing yours, gives you a huge winning edge. *An absolute must buy!* $59.95.

CARO'S MAJOR POKER SEMINAR

The legendary "Mad Genius" is at it again, giving poker advice in VHS format. This new tape is based on the inaugural class at Mike Caro University of Poker, Gaming and Life strategy. The material given on this tape is based on many fundamentals introduced in Caro's books, papers, and articles and is prepared in such a way that reinforces concepts old and new. Caro's style is easy-going but intense with key concepts stressed and repeated. This tape will improve your play. 60 Minutes. $24.95.

CARO'S POWER POKER SEMINAR

This powerful video shows you how to win big money using the little-known concepts of world champion players. This advice will be worth thousands of dollars to you every year, even more if you're a big money player! After 15 years of refusing to allow his seminars to be filmed, Caro presents entertaining but serious coverage of his long-guarded secrets. Contains the most profitable poker advice ever put on video. 62 Minutes! $39.95.